Daily Digs

Daily Journal for Volleyball Coaches and Players

by Jackie Taylor

Dedication

This journal is dedicated to all Christ-followers who love volleyball and desire to improve their spiritual and personal growth while preserving a record of the many blessings, trials, and relationships God has used to develop them on their journey through life.

Acknowledgments

First, I would like to thank my husband, Greg Taylor, for encouraging me to pursue my dreams. I would like to thank my son, Jacob, and my daughter, Jenna, for sharing their mom with so many athletes through the years. Thanks to my mother, Alice Morrison, for always believing in me. Thanks to my father, Johnny Barger, for instilling a love of sports in me.

Lastly, I would like to thank the Fellowship of Christian Athletes and the coaches of Northside High School in Columbus, Georgia for allowing me to serve as Team Chaplain for the Lady Patriots volleyball team. These ladies inspire me to create tools to help them succeed in life.

How to Use the Journal:

This 365-day journal is specifically designed with the volleyball coach or athlete in mind. It is centered around basic concepts very familiar to anyone who spends time on the court.

The Serve
The importance of a proper serve cannot be denied. Players who execute accurate serves increase the likelihood of their team's success. The best way to get into the proper service position is to start your day off with the greatest playbook in existence, God's Word. Let the Holy Spirit direct you by using the SERVE method below:

SCRIPTURE— What Scripture reference(s) are you reading?

EMPHASIS— What did the Holy Spirit emphasize to you as you read? (If nothing, you haven't read long enough.)

REPENT— What do you need to turn away from so that you may DO what you read?

VOLLEY— What are some ways to share what you've learned with others?

EXPRESS— Express your praise, your confession, your requests to the Lord.

The Lineup
A volleyball lineup lists the serving order and the players' starting positions on the court. Your lineup should reflect the order in which you need to get things done. The goal is to accomplish the tasks in your lineup each day.

The Score Sheet
At the end of the day, the athlete or coach will give the "score" of that day's accomplishments, thoughts, and events. In the future, when you look back at these recaps, you will be reminded of what God has done for you.

This journal is your personal history book. Enjoy the journey!

__Go__ into *__All__* the world, *__Make__* disciples, *__Empowered__* from on high.

Date:_____

SCRIPTURE—What Scripture reference(s) are you reading?

_____

EMPHASIS—What did the Holy Spirit emphasize to you as you read? (If nothing, you haven't read long enough.)

_____
_____
_____
_____
_____
_____

REPENT—What do you need to turn away from so that you may DO what you read?

_____
_____
_____
_____
_____

VOLLEY—What are some ways to share what you've learned with others?

_____
_____

EXPRESS—Express your praise, your confession, your requests to the Lord.

_____
_____
_____
_____
_____
_____
_____
_____
_____
_____
_____

__Go__ into __All__ the world, __Make__ disciples, __Empowered__ from on high.

The Lineup

(What needs to be accomplished today?)

1. _____
2. _____
3. _____
4. _____
5. _____
6. _____

Subs:

_____

_____

"teach me to number my days"

24 Hours

SCORE SHEET (Recap of the day)

_____
_____
_____
_____
_____
_____
_____
_____
_____
_____
_____
_____
_____
_____
_____

__Go__ into *__All__* the world, *__Make__* disciples, *__Empowered__* from on high.

Date:_____

SCRIPTURE—What Scripture reference(s) are you reading?

_____

EMPHASIS—What did the Holy Spirit emphasize to you as you read? (If nothing, you haven't read long enough.)

_____
_____
_____
_____
_____
_____

REPENT—What do you need to turn away from so that you may DO what you read?

_____
_____
_____
_____
_____

VOLLEY—What are some ways to share what you've learned with others?

_____
_____

EXPRESS—Express your praise, your confession, your requests to the Lord.

_____
_____
_____
_____
_____
_____
_____
_____
_____
_____
_____
_____

__Go__ into __All__ the world, __Make__ disciples, __Empowered__ from on high.

The Lineup

(What needs to be accomplished today?)

1. _____
2. _____
3. _____
4. _____
5. _____
6. _____

Subs:

_____

_____

"teach me to number my days"

24 Hours

SCORE SHEET (Recap of the day)

_____
_____
_____
_____
_____
_____
_____
_____
_____
_____
_____
_____
_____
_____
_____

__Go__ into __All__ the world, __Make__ disciples, __Empowered__ from on high.

Date:_____

S CRIPTURE—What Scripture reference(s) are you reading?

_____

E MPHASIS—What did the Holy Spirit emphasize to you as you read? (If nothing, you haven't read long enough.)

_____
_____
_____
_____
_____
_____

R EPENT—What do you need to turn away from so that you may DO what you read?

_____
_____
_____
_____
_____

V OLLEY—What are some ways to share what you've learned with others?

_____
_____

E XPRESS—Express your praise, your confession, your requests to the Lord.

_____
_____
_____
_____
_____
_____
_____
_____
_____
_____
_____
_____

__Go__ into __All__ the world, __Make__ disciples, __Empowered__ from on high.

The Lineup

(What needs to be accomplished today?)

1. _____
2. _____
3. _____
4. _____
5. _____
6. _____

Subs:

_____

_____

"teach me to number my days"

24 Hours

SCORE SHEET (Recap of the day)

_____
_____
_____
_____
_____
_____
_____
_____
_____
_____
_____
_____
_____
_____
_____
_____

__Go__ into __All__ the world, __Make__ disciples, __Empowered__ from on high.

Date:_____

SCRIPTURE—What Scripture reference(s) are you reading?

_____

EMPHASIS—What did the Holy Spirit emphasize to you as you read? (If nothing, you haven't read long enough.)

_____
_____
_____
_____
_____
_____

REPENT—What do you need to turn away from so that you may DO what you read?

_____
_____
_____
_____
_____

VOLLEY—What are some ways to share what you've learned with others?

_____
_____

EXPRESS—Express your praise, your confession, your requests to the Lord.

_____
_____
_____
_____
_____
_____
_____
_____
_____
_____
_____
_____

__Go__ into __All__ the world, __Make__ disciples, __Empowered__ from on high.

The Lineup

(What needs to be accomplished today?)

1. _____
2. _____
3. _____
4. _____
5. _____
6. _____

Subs:

_____

_____

"teach me to number my days"

24 Hours

SCORE SHEET (Recap of the day)

_____
_____
_____
_____
_____
_____
_____
_____
_____
_____
_____
_____
_____
_____

__Go__ into __All__ the world, __Make__ disciples, __Empowered__ from on high.

Date:_____

SCRIPTURE—What Scripture reference(s) are you reading?

_____

EMPHASIS—What did the Holy Spirit emphasize to you as you read? (If nothing, you haven't read long enough.)

_____
_____
_____
_____
_____
_____

REPENT—What do you need to turn away from so that you may DO what you read?

_____
_____
_____
_____
_____

VOLLEY—What are some ways to share what you've learned with others?

_____
_____

EXPRESS—Express your praise, your confession, your requests to the Lord.

_____
_____
_____
_____
_____
_____
_____
_____
_____
_____
_____
_____

Go into *All* the world, *Make* disciples, *Empowered* from on high.

The Lineup

(What needs to be accomplished today?)

1. _____
2. _____
3. _____
4. _____
5. _____
6. _____

Subs:

_____

_____

"teach me to number my days"

24 Hours

SCORE SHEET (Recap of the day)

_____
_____
_____
_____
_____
_____
_____
_____
_____
_____
_____
_____
_____
_____
_____

__Go__ into __All__ the world, __Make__ disciples, __Empowered__ from on high.

Date:_____

SCRIPTURE—What Scripture reference(s) are you reading?

_____

EMPHASIS—What did the Holy Spirit emphasize to you as you read? (If nothing, you haven't read long enough.)

_____
_____
_____
_____
_____
_____

REPENT—What do you need to turn away from so that you may DO what you read?

_____
_____
_____
_____
_____

VOLLEY—What are some ways to share what you've learned with others?

_____
_____

EXPRESS—Express your praise, your confession, your requests to the Lord.

_____
_____
_____
_____
_____
_____
_____
_____
_____
_____
_____

**Go** into **All** the world, **Make** disciples, **Empowered** from on high.

The Lineup

(What needs to be accomplished today?)

1. _____
2. _____
3. _____
4. _____
5. _____
6. _____

Subs:

_____

_____

"teach me to number my days"

24 Hours

SCORE SHEET (Recap of the day)

_____
_____
_____
_____
_____
_____
_____
_____
_____
_____
_____
_____
_____
_____
_____

***Go** into **All** the world, **Make** disciples, **Empowered** from on high.*

Date:_____

SCRIPTURE—What Scripture reference(s) are you reading?

_____

EMPHASIS—What did the Holy Spirit emphasize to you as you read? (If nothing, you haven't read long enough.)

_____
_____
_____
_____
_____
_____

REPENT—What do you need to turn away from so that you may DO what you read?

_____
_____
_____
_____
_____

VOLLEY—What are some ways to share what you've learned with others?

_____
_____

EXPRESS—Express your praise, your confession, your requests to the Lord.

_____
_____
_____
_____
_____
_____
_____
_____
_____
_____
_____
_____

Go into *All* the world, *Make* disciples, *Empowered* from on high.

The Lineup

(What needs to be accomplished today?)

1. _____
2. _____
3. _____
4. _____
5. _____
6. _____

Subs:

_____

_____

"teach me to number my days" — 24 Hours

SCORE SHEET (Recap of the day)

_____
_____
_____
_____
_____
_____
_____
_____
_____
_____
_____
_____
_____
_____
_____

__Go__ into __All__ the world, __Make__ disciples, __Empowered__ from on high.

Date:_____

SCRIPTURE—What Scripture reference(s) are you reading?

_____

EMPHASIS—What did the Holy Spirit emphasize to you as you read? (If nothing, you haven't read long enough.)

_____
_____
_____
_____
_____
_____

REPENT—What do you need to turn away from so that you may DO what you read?

_____
_____
_____
_____
_____

VOLLEY—What are some ways to share what you've learned with others?

_____
_____

EXPRESS—Express your praise, your confession, your requests to the Lord.

_____
_____
_____
_____
_____
_____
_____
_____
_____
_____
_____
_____

__Go__ into __All__ the world, __Make__ disciples, __Empowered__ from on high.

The Lineup

(What needs to be accomplished today?)

1. _____

2. _____

3. _____

4. _____

5. _____

6. _____

Subs:

_____

_____

"teach me to number my days"

24 Hours

SCORE SHEET (Recap of the day)

_____
_____
_____
_____
_____
_____
_____
_____
_____
_____
_____
_____
_____
_____

__Go__ into __All__ the world, __Make__ disciples, __Empowered__ from on high.

Date:_____

SCRIPTURE—What Scripture reference(s) are you reading?

_____

EMPHASIS—What did the Holy Spirit emphasize to you as you read? (If nothing, you haven't read long enough.)

_____
_____
_____
_____
_____
_____

REPENT—What do you need to turn away from so that you may DO what you read?

_____
_____
_____
_____
_____

VOLLEY—What are some ways to share what you've learned with others?

_____
_____

EXPRESS—Express your praise, your confession, your requests to the Lord.

_____
_____
_____
_____
_____
_____
_____
_____
_____
_____
_____
_____

__Go__ into __All__ the world, __Make__ disciples, __Empowered__ from on high.

The Lineup

(What needs to be accomplished today?)

1. _____

2. _____

3. _____

4. _____

5. _____

6. _____

Subs:

_____

_____

SCORE SHEET (Recap of the day)

_____
_____
_____
_____
_____
_____
_____
_____
_____
_____
_____
_____
_____
_____

__Go__ into __All__ the world, __Make__ disciples, __Empowered__ from on high.

Date:_____

SCRIPTURE—What Scripture reference(s) are you reading?

_____

EMPHASIS—What did the Holy Spirit emphasize to you as you read? (If nothing, you haven't read long enough.)

_____
_____
_____
_____
_____
_____

REPENT—What do you need to turn away from so that you may DO what you read?

_____
_____
_____
_____
_____

VOLLEY—What are some ways to share what you've learned with others?

_____
_____

EXPRESS—Express your praise, your confession, your requests to the Lord.

_____
_____
_____
_____
_____
_____
_____
_____
_____
_____
_____
_____

__Go__ into __All__ the world, __Make__ disciples, __Empowered__ from on high.

The Lineup

(What needs to be accomplished today?)

1. _____
2. _____
3. _____
4. _____
5. _____
6. _____

Subs:

_____

_____

"teach me to number my days"

24 Hours

SCORE SHEET (Recap of the day)

_____
_____
_____
_____
_____
_____
_____
_____
_____
_____
_____
_____
_____
_____

Go into ***All*** the world, ***Make*** disciples, ***Empowered*** from on high.

Date:_____

Sᴄʀɪᴘᴛᴜʀᴇ—What Scripture reference(s) are you reading?

_____

Eᴍᴘʜᴀsɪs—What did the Holy Spirit emphasize to you as you read? (If nothing, you haven't read long enough.)

_____
_____
_____
_____
_____
_____

Rᴇᴘᴇɴᴛ—What do you need to turn away from so that you may DO what you read?

_____
_____
_____
_____
_____

Vᴏʟʟᴇʏ—What are some ways to share what you've learned with others?

_____
_____

Exᴘʀᴇss—Express your praise, your confession, your requests to the Lord.

_____
_____
_____
_____
_____
_____
_____
_____
_____
_____
_____

***Go** into **All** the world, **Make** disciples, **Empowered** from on high.*

The Lineup

(What needs to be accomplished today?)

1. _____

2. _____

3. _____

4. _____

5. _____

6. _____

Subs:

_____

_____

"teach me to number my days"

24 Hours

SCORE SHEET (Recap of the day)

_____
_____
_____
_____
_____
_____
_____
_____
_____
_____
_____
_____
_____
_____

__Go__ into __All__ the world, __Make__ disciples, __Empowered__ from on high.

Date:_____

SCRIPTURE—What Scripture reference(s) are you reading?

_____

EMPHASIS—What did the Holy Spirit emphasize to you as you read? (If nothing, you haven't read long enough.)

_____
_____
_____
_____
_____
_____

REPENT—What do you need to turn away from so that you may DO what you read?

_____
_____
_____
_____
_____

VOLLEY—What are some ways to share what you've learned with others?

_____
_____

EXPRESS—Express your praise, your confession, your requests to the Lord.

_____
_____
_____
_____
_____
_____
_____
_____
_____
_____
_____
_____

__Go__ into __All__ the world, __Make__ disciples, __Empowered__ from on high.

The Lineup

(What needs to be accomplished today?)

1. _____

2. _____

3. _____

4. _____

5. _____

6. _____

Subs:

_____

_____

"teach me to number my days"

24 Hours

SCORE SHEET (Recap of the day)

_____
_____
_____
_____
_____
_____
_____
_____
_____
_____
_____
_____
_____
_____
_____

__Go__ into *__All__* the world, *__Make__* disciples, *__Empowered__* from on high.

Date:_____

SCRIPTURE—What Scripture reference(s) are you reading?

_____

EMPHASIS—What did the Holy Spirit emphasize to you as you read? (If nothing, you haven't read long enough.)

_____
_____
_____
_____
_____
_____

REPENT—What do you need to turn away from so that you may DO what you read?

_____
_____
_____
_____
_____

VOLLEY—What are some ways to share what you've learned with others?

_____
_____

EXPRESS—Express your praise, your confession, your requests to the Lord.

_____
_____
_____
_____
_____
_____
_____
_____
_____
_____
_____
_____

__Go__ into __All__ the world, __Make__ disciples, __Empowered__ from on high.

The Lineup

(What needs to be accomplished today?)

1. _____
2. _____
3. _____
4. _____
5. _____
6. _____

Subs:

_____

_____

"teach me to number my days"

24 Hours

SCORE SHEET (Recap of the day)

_____
_____
_____
_____
_____
_____
_____
_____
_____
_____
_____
_____
_____
_____
_____
_____

<u>**Go**</u> into <u>**All**</u> the world, <u>**Make**</u> disciples, <u>**Empowered**</u> from on high.

Date:_____

Sᴄʀɪᴘᴛᴜʀᴇ—What Scripture reference(s) are you reading?

_____

Eᴍᴘʜᴀsɪs—What did the Holy Spirit emphasize to you as you read? (If nothing, you haven't read long enough.)

_____
_____
_____
_____
_____
_____

Rᴇᴘᴇɴᴛ—What do you need to turn away from so that you may DO what you read?

_____
_____
_____
_____
_____

Vᴏʟʟᴇʏ—What are some ways to share what you've learned with others?

_____
_____

Eхᴘʀᴇss—Express your praise, your confession, your requests to the Lord.

_____
_____
_____
_____
_____
_____
_____
_____
_____
_____
_____

**Go** into **All** the world, **Make** disciples, **Empowered** from on high.

The Lineup

(What needs to be accomplished today?)

1. _____

2. _____

3. _____

4. _____

5. _____

6. _____

Subs:

_____

_____

SCORE SHEET (Recap of the day)

_____
_____
_____
_____
_____
_____
_____
_____
_____
_____
_____
_____
_____
_____

Go into *All* the world, *Make* disciples, *Empowered* from on high.

Date:_____

SCRIPTURE—What Scripture reference(s) are you reading?

_____

EMPHASIS—What did the Holy Spirit emphasize to you as you read? (If nothing, you haven't read long enough.)

_____
_____
_____
_____
_____
_____

REPENT—What do you need to turn away from so that you may DO what you read?

_____
_____
_____
_____
_____

VOLLEY—What are some ways to share what you've learned with others?

_____
_____

EXPRESS—Express your praise, your confession, your requests to the Lord.

_____
_____
_____
_____
_____
_____
_____
_____
_____
_____
_____

__Go__ into __All__ the world, __Make__ disciples, __Empowered__ from on high.

The Lineup

(What needs to be accomplished today?)

1. _____
2. _____
3. _____
4. _____
5. _____
6. _____

Subs:

_____

_____

"teach me to number my days"

24 Hours

SCORE SHEET (Recap of the day)

_____
_____
_____
_____
_____
_____
_____
_____
_____
_____
_____
_____
_____
_____
_____

Go into ***All*** the world, ***Make*** disciples, ***Empowered*** from on high.

Date:_____

SCRIPTURE—What Scripture reference(s) are you reading?

_____

EMPHASIS—What did the Holy Spirit emphasize to you as you read? (If nothing, you haven't read long enough.)

_____
_____
_____
_____
_____
_____

REPENT—What do you need to turn away from so that you may DO what you read?

_____
_____
_____
_____
_____

VOLLEY—What are some ways to share what you've learned with others?

_____
_____

EXPRESS—Express your praise, your confession, your requests to the Lord.

_____
_____
_____
_____
_____
_____
_____
_____
_____
_____
_____
_____

__Go__ into __All__ the world, __Make__ disciples, __Empowered__ from on high.

The Lineup

(What needs to be accomplished today?)

1. _____
2. _____
3. _____
4. _____
5. _____
6. _____

Subs:

_____

_____

SCORE SHEET (Recap of the day)

_____
_____
_____
_____
_____
_____
_____
_____
_____
_____
_____
_____
_____
_____
_____

__Go__ into __All__ the world, __Make__ disciples, __Empowered__ from on high.

Date:_____

SCRIPTURE—What Scripture reference(s) are you reading?

_____

EMPHASIS—What did the Holy Spirit emphasize to you as you read? (If nothing, you haven't read long enough.)

_____
_____
_____
_____
_____
_____

REPENT—What do you need to turn away from so that you may DO what you read?

_____
_____
_____
_____
_____

VOLLEY—What are some ways to share what you've learned with others?

_____
_____

EXPRESS—Express your praise, your confession, your requests to the Lord.

_____
_____
_____
_____
_____
_____
_____
_____
_____
_____
_____
_____
_____

__Go__ into __All__ the world, __Make__ disciples, __Empowered__ from on high.

The Lineup

(What needs to be accomplished today?)

1. _____
2. _____
3. _____
4. _____
5. _____
6. _____

Subs:

_____

_____

"teach me to number my days"

24 Hours

SCORE SHEET (Recap of the day)

_____
_____
_____
_____
_____
_____
_____
_____
_____
_____
_____
_____
_____
_____
_____

__Go__ into __All__ the world, __Make__ disciples, __Empowered__ from on high.

Date:_____

SCRIPTURE—What Scripture reference(s) are you reading?

_____

EMPHASIS—What did the Holy Spirit emphasize to you as you read? (If nothing, you haven't read long enough.)

_____
_____
_____
_____
_____
_____

REPENT—What do you need to turn away from so that you may DO what you read?

_____
_____
_____
_____
_____

VOLLEY—What are some ways to share what you've learned with others?

_____
_____

EXPRESS—Express your praise, your confession, your requests to the Lord.

_____
_____
_____
_____
_____
_____
_____
_____
_____
_____
_____

__Go__ into __All__ the world, __Make__ disciples, __Empowered__ from on high.

The Lineup

(What needs to be accomplished today?)

1. _____
2. _____
3. _____
4. _____
5. _____
6. _____

Subs:

_____

_____

"teach me to number my days"

24 Hours

SCORE SHEET (Recap of the day)

_____
_____
_____
_____
_____
_____
_____
_____
_____
_____
_____
_____
_____
_____

__Go__ into __All__ the world, __Make__ disciples, __Empowered__ from on high.

Date:_____

SCRIPTURE—What Scripture reference(s) are you reading?

_____

EMPHASIS—What did the Holy Spirit emphasize to you as you read? (If nothing, you haven't read long enough.)

_____
_____
_____
_____
_____
_____

REPENT—What do you need to turn away from so that you may DO what you read?

_____
_____
_____
_____
_____

VOLLEY—What are some ways to share what you've learned with others?

_____
_____

EXPRESS—Express your praise, your confession, your requests to the Lord.

_____
_____
_____
_____
_____
_____
_____
_____
_____
_____
_____

__Go__ into __All__ the world, __Make__ disciples, __Empowered__ from on high.

The Lineup

(What needs to be accomplished today?)

1. _____
2. _____
3. _____
4. _____
5. _____
6. _____

Subs:

_____

_____

"teach me to number my days"

24 Hours

SCORE SHEET (Recap of the day)

_____
_____
_____
_____
_____
_____
_____
_____
_____
_____
_____
_____
_____
_____

__Go__ into __All__ the world, __Make__ disciples, __Empowered__ from on high.

Date:_____

S CRIPTURE—What Scripture reference(s) are you reading?

_____

E MPHASIS—What did the Holy Spirit emphasize to you as you read? (If nothing, you haven't read long enough.)

_____
_____
_____
_____
_____
_____

R EPENT—What do you need to turn away from so that you may DO what you read?

_____
_____
_____
_____
_____

V OLLEY—What are some ways to share what you've learned with others?

_____
_____

E XPRESS—Express your praise, your confession, your requests to the Lord.

_____
_____
_____
_____
_____
_____
_____
_____
_____
_____
_____
_____

__Go__ into __All__ the world, __Make__ disciples, __Empowered__ from on high.

The Lineup

(What needs to be accomplished today?)

1. _____

2. _____

3. _____

4. _____

5. _____

6. _____

Subs:

_____

_____

"teach me to number my days"

24 Hours

SCORE SHEET (Recap of the day)

_____

_____

_____

_____

_____

_____

_____

_____

_____

_____

_____

_____

_____

_____

_____

Go into ***All*** the world, ***Make*** disciples, ***Empowered*** from on high.

Date:_____

SCRIPTURE—What Scripture reference(s) are you reading?

_____

EMPHASIS—What did the Holy Spirit emphasize to you as you read? (If nothing, you haven't read long enough.)

_____
_____
_____
_____
_____
_____

REPENT—What do you need to turn away from so that you may DO what you read?

_____
_____
_____
_____
_____

VOLLEY—What are some ways to share what you've learned with others?

_____
_____

EXPRESS—Express your praise, your confession, your requests to the Lord.

_____
_____
_____
_____
_____
_____
_____
_____
_____
_____
_____
_____

__Go__ into __All__ the world, __Make__ disciples, __Empowered__ from on high.

The Lineup

(What needs to be accomplished today?)

1. _____
2. _____
3. _____
4. _____
5. _____
6. _____

Subs:

_____

_____

"teach me to number my days"

24 Hours

SCORE SHEET (Recap of the day)

_____
_____
_____
_____
_____
_____
_____
_____
_____
_____
_____
_____
_____
_____

__Go__ into __All__ the world, __Make__ disciples, __Empowered__ from on high.

Date:_____

SCRIPTURE—What Scripture reference(s) are you reading?

_____

EMPHASIS—What did the Holy Spirit emphasize to you as you read? (If nothing, you haven't read long enough.)

_____
_____
_____
_____
_____
_____

REPENT—What do you need to turn away from so that you may DO what you read?

_____
_____
_____
_____

VOLLEY—What are some ways to share what you've learned with others?

_____
_____

EXPRESS—Express your praise, your confession, your requests to the Lord.

_____
_____
_____
_____
_____
_____
_____
_____
_____
_____
_____

**Go** into **All** the world, **Make** disciples, **Empowered** from on high.

The Lineup

(What needs to be accomplished today?)

1. _____
2. _____
3. _____
4. _____
5. _____
6. _____

Subs:

_____

_____

"teach me to number my days"

24 Hours

SCORE SHEET (Recap of the day)

_____
_____
_____
_____
_____
_____
_____
_____
_____
_____
_____
_____
_____
_____
_____
_____

_**Go**_ into _**All**_ the world, _**Make**_ disciples, _**Empowered**_ from on high.

Date:_____

SCRIPTURE—What Scripture reference(s) are you reading?

_____

EMPHASIS—What did the Holy Spirit emphasize to you as you read? (If nothing, you haven't read long enough.)

_____
_____
_____
_____
_____
_____

REPENT—What do you need to turn away from so that you may DO what you read?

_____
_____
_____
_____
_____

VOLLEY—What are some ways to share what you've learned with others?

_____
_____

EXPRESS—Express your praise, your confession, your requests to the Lord.

_____
_____
_____
_____
_____
_____
_____
_____
_____
_____
_____
_____

__Go__ into __All__ the world, __Make__ disciples, __Empowered__ from on high.

The Lineup

(What needs to be accomplished today?)

1. _____

2. _____

3. _____

4. _____

5. _____

6. _____

Subs:

_____

_____

"teach me to number my days"

24 Hours

SCORE SHEET (Recap of the day)

_____
_____
_____
_____
_____
_____
_____
_____
_____
_____
_____
_____
_____
_____

**Go** into **All** the world, **Make** disciples, **Empowered** from on high.

Date:_____

SCRIPTURE—What Scripture reference(s) are you reading?

_____

EMPHASIS—What did the Holy Spirit emphasize to you as you read? (If nothing, you haven't read long enough.)

_____
_____
_____
_____
_____
_____

REPENT—What do you need to turn away from so that you may DO what you read?

_____
_____
_____
_____
_____

VOLLEY—What are some ways to share what you've learned with others?

_____
_____

EXPRESS—Express your praise, your confession, your requests to the Lord.

_____
_____
_____
_____
_____
_____
_____
_____
_____
_____
_____

__Go__ into __All__ the world, __Make__ disciples, __Empowered__ from on high.

The Lineup

(What needs to be accomplished today?)

1. _____
2. _____
3. _____
4. _____
5. _____
6. _____

Subs:

_____

_____

"teach me to number my days"

24 Hours

SCORE SHEET (Recap of the day)

_____
_____
_____
_____
_____
_____
_____
_____
_____
_____
_____
_____
_____
_____
_____

_**Go**_ into _**All**_ the world, _**Make**_ disciples, _**Empowered**_ from on high.

Date:_____

SCRIPTURE—What Scripture reference(s) are you reading?

_____

EMPHASIS—What did the Holy Spirit emphasize to you as you read? (If nothing, you haven't read long enough.)

_____
_____
_____
_____
_____
_____

REPENT—What do you need to turn away from so that you may DO what you read?

_____
_____
_____
_____
_____

VOLLEY—What are some ways to share what you've learned with others?

_____
_____

EXPRESS—Express your praise, your confession, your requests to the Lord.

_____
_____
_____
_____
_____
_____
_____
_____
_____
_____
_____

__Go__ into *__All__* the world, *__Make__* disciples, *__Empowered__* from on high.

The Lineup

(What needs to be accomplished today?)

1. _____
2. _____
3. _____
4. _____
5. _____
6. _____

Subs:

_____

_____

"teach me to number my days"

24 Hours

SCORE SHEET (Recap of the day)

_____
_____
_____
_____
_____
_____
_____
_____
_____
_____
_____
_____
_____
_____
_____

__Go__ into __All__ the world, __Make__ disciples, __Empowered__ from on high.

Date:_____

SCRIPTURE—What Scripture reference(s) are you reading?

_____

EMPHASIS—What did the Holy Spirit emphasize to you as you read? (If nothing, you haven't read long enough.)

_____
_____
_____
_____
_____
_____

REPENT—What do you need to turn away from so that you may DO what you read?

_____
_____
_____
_____
_____

VOLLEY—What are some ways to share what you've learned with others?

_____
_____

EXPRESS—Express your praise, your confession, your requests to the Lord.

_____
_____
_____
_____
_____
_____
_____
_____
_____
_____
_____
_____

_**Go**_ into _**All**_ the world, _**Make**_ disciples, _**Empowered**_ from on high.

The Lineup

(What needs to be accomplished today?)

1. _____

2. _____

3. _____

4. _____

5. _____

6. _____

Subs:

_____

_____

"teach me to number my days"

24 Hours

SCORE SHEET (Recap of the day)

_____
_____
_____
_____
_____
_____
_____
_____
_____
_____
_____
_____
_____
_____
_____

**Go** into **All** the world, **Make** disciples, **Empowered** from on high.

Date:_____

SCRIPTURE—What Scripture reference(s) are you reading?

_____

EMPHASIS—What did the Holy Spirit emphasize to you as you read? (If nothing, you haven't read long enough.)

_____
_____
_____
_____
_____
_____

REPENT—What do you need to turn away from so that you may DO what you read?

_____
_____
_____
_____
_____

VOLLEY—What are some ways to share what you've learned with others?

_____
_____

EXPRESS—Express your praise, your confession, your requests to the Lord.

_____
_____
_____
_____
_____
_____
_____
_____
_____
_____
_____

__Go__ into __All__ the world, __Make__ disciples, __Empowered__ from on high.

The Lineup

(What needs to be accomplished today?)

1. _____
2. _____
3. _____
4. _____
5. _____
6. _____

Subs:

_____

_____

"teach me to number my days"

24 Hours

SCORE SHEET (Recap of the day)

_____
_____
_____
_____
_____
_____
_____
_____
_____
_____
_____
_____
_____
_____
_____

__Go__ into __All__ the world, __Make__ disciples, __Empowered__ from on high.

Date:_____

SCRIPTURE—What Scripture reference(s) are you reading?

_____

EMPHASIS—What did the Holy Spirit emphasize to you as you read? (If nothing, you haven't read long enough.)

_____
_____
_____
_____
_____
_____

REPENT—What do you need to turn away from so that you may DO what you read?

_____
_____
_____
_____
_____

VOLLEY—What are some ways to share what you've learned with others?

_____
_____

EXPRESS—Express your praise, your confession, your requests to the Lord.

_____
_____
_____
_____
_____
_____
_____
_____
_____
_____
_____
_____

__Go__ into __All__ the world, __Make__ disciples, __Empowered__ from on high.

The Lineup

(What needs to be accomplished today?)

1. _____

2. _____

3. _____

4. _____

5. _____

6. _____

Subs:

_____

_____

"teach me to number my days"

24 Hours

SCORE SHEET (Recap of the day)

_____
_____
_____
_____
_____
_____
_____
_____
_____
_____
_____
_____
_____
_____

**Go** into **All** the world, **Make** disciples, **Empowered** from on high.

Date:_____

SCRIPTURE—What Scripture reference(s) are you reading?

_____

EMPHASIS—What did the Holy Spirit emphasize to you as you read? (If nothing, you haven't read long enough.)

_____
_____
_____
_____
_____
_____

REPENT—What do you need to turn away from so that you may DO what you read?

_____
_____
_____
_____
_____

VOLLEY—What are some ways to share what you've learned with others?

_____
_____

EXPRESS—Express your praise, your confession, your requests to the Lord.

_____
_____
_____
_____
_____
_____
_____
_____
_____
_____
_____
_____

__Go__ into __All__ the world, __Make__ disciples, __Empowered__ from on high.

The Lineup

(What needs to be accomplished today?)

1. _____

2. _____

3. _____

4. _____

5. _____

6. _____

Subs:

_____

_____

"teach me to number my days" 24 Hours

SCORE SHEET (Recap of the day)

_____
_____
_____
_____
_____
_____
_____
_____
_____
_____
_____
_____
_____
_____
_____
_____

__Go__ into *__All__* the world, *__Make__* disciples, *__Empowered__* from on high.

Date:_____

SCRIPTURE—What Scripture reference(s) are you reading?

_____

EMPHASIS—What did the Holy Spirit emphasize to you as you read? (If nothing, you haven't read long enough.)

_____
_____
_____
_____
_____
_____

REPENT—What do you need to turn away from so that you may DO what you read?

_____
_____
_____
_____
_____

VOLLEY—What are some ways to share what you've learned with others?

_____
_____

EXPRESS—Express your praise, your confession, your requests to the Lord.

_____
_____
_____
_____
_____
_____
_____
_____
_____
_____
_____

__Go__ into __All__ the world, __Make__ disciples, __Empowered__ from on high.

The Lineup

(What needs to be accomplished today?)

1. _____
2. _____
3. _____
4. _____
5. _____
6. _____

Subs:

_____

_____

"teach me to number my days"

24 Hours

SCORE SHEET (Recap of the day)

_____
_____
_____
_____
_____
_____
_____
_____
_____
_____
_____
_____
_____
_____
_____

**Go** into **All** the world, **Make** disciples, **Empowered** from on high.

Date:_____

SCRIPTURE—What Scripture reference(s) are you reading?

_____

EMPHASIS—What did the Holy Spirit emphasize to you as you read? (If nothing, you haven't read long enough.)

_____
_____
_____
_____
_____
_____

REPENT—What do you need to turn away from so that you may DO what you read?

_____
_____
_____
_____
_____

VOLLEY—What are some ways to share what you've learned with others?

_____
_____

EXPRESS—Express your praise, your confession, your requests to the Lord.

_____
_____
_____
_____
_____
_____
_____
_____
_____
_____
_____
_____

_**Go**_ into _**All**_ the world, _**Make**_ disciples, _**Empowered**_ from on high.

The Lineup

(What needs to be accomplished today?)

1. _____
2. _____
3. _____
4. _____
5. _____
6. _____

Subs:

_____

_____

"teach me to number my days"

24 Hours

SCORE SHEET (Recap of the day)

_____
_____
_____
_____
_____
_____
_____
_____
_____
_____
_____
_____
_____
_____

__Go__ into __All__ the world, __Make__ disciples, __Empowered__ from on high.

Date:_____

SCRIPTURE—What Scripture reference(s) are you reading?

_____

EMPHASIS—What did the Holy Spirit emphasize to you as you read? (If nothing, you haven't read long enough.)

_____
_____
_____
_____
_____
_____

REPENT—What do you need to turn away from so that you may DO what you read?

_____
_____
_____
_____
_____

VOLLEY—What are some ways to share what you've learned with others?

_____
_____

EXPRESS—Express your praise, your confession, your requests to the Lord.

_____
_____
_____
_____
_____
_____
_____
_____
_____
_____
_____
_____

__Go__ into __All__ the world, __Make__ disciples, __Empowered__ from on high.

The Lineup

(What needs to be accomplished today?)

1. _____

2. _____

3. _____

4. _____

5. _____

6. _____

Subs:

_____

_____

"teach me to number my days"

24 Hours

SCORE SHEET (Recap of the day)

_____

_____

_____

_____

_____

_____

_____

_____

_____

_____

_____

_____

_____

_**Go**_ into _**All**_ the world, _**Make**_ disciples, _**Empowered**_ from on high.

Date:_____

SCRIPTURE—What Scripture reference(s) are you reading?

_____

EMPHASIS—What did the Holy Spirit emphasize to you as you read? (If nothing, you haven't read long enough.)

_____
_____
_____
_____
_____
_____

REPENT—What do you need to turn away from so that you may DO what you read?

_____
_____
_____
_____
_____

VOLLEY—What are some ways to share what you've learned with others?

_____
_____

EXPRESS—Express your praise, your confession, your requests to the Lord.

_____
_____
_____
_____
_____
_____
_____
_____
_____
_____
_____

__Go__ into __All__ the world, __Make__ disciples, __Empowered__ from on high.

The Lineup

(What needs to be accomplished today?)

1. _____
2. _____
3. _____
4. _____
5. _____
6. _____

Subs:

_____

_____

"teach me to number my days"

24 Hours

SCORE SHEET (Recap of the day)

_____
_____
_____
_____
_____
_____
_____
_____
_____
_____
_____
_____
_____
_____
_____
_____

**Go** into **All** the world, **Make** disciples, **Empowered** from on high.

Date:_____

SCRIPTURE—What Scripture reference(s) are you reading?

_____

EMPHASIS—What did the Holy Spirit emphasize to you as you read? (If nothing, you haven't read long enough.)

_____
_____
_____
_____
_____
_____

REPENT—What do you need to turn away from so that you may DO what you read?

_____
_____
_____
_____
_____

VOLLEY—What are some ways to share what you've learned with others?

_____
_____

EXPRESS—Express your praise, your confession, your requests to the Lord.

_____
_____
_____
_____
_____
_____
_____
_____
_____
_____
_____
_____

__Go__ into __All__ the world, __Make__ disciples, __Empowered__ from on high.

The Lineup

(What needs to be accomplished today?)

1. _____
2. _____
3. _____
4. _____
5. _____
6. _____

Subs:

_____

_____

"teach me to number my days"

24 Hours

SCORE SHEET (Recap of the day)

_____
_____
_____
_____
_____
_____
_____
_____
_____
_____
_____
_____
_____
_____

__Go__ into __All__ the world, __Make__ disciples, __Empowered__ from on high.

Date:_____

SCRIPTURE—What Scripture reference(s) are you reading?

_____

EMPHASIS—What did the Holy Spirit emphasize to you as you read? (If nothing, you haven't read long enough.)

_____
_____
_____
_____
_____
_____

REPENT—What do you need to turn away from so that you may DO what you read?

_____
_____
_____
_____
_____

VOLLEY—What are some ways to share what you've learned with others?

_____
_____

EXPRESS—Express your praise, your confession, your requests to the Lord.

_____
_____
_____
_____
_____
_____
_____
_____
_____
_____
_____
_____

__Go__ into __All__ the world, __Make__ disciples, __Empowered__ from on high.

The Lineup

(What needs to be accomplished today?)

1. _____
2. _____
3. _____
4. _____
5. _____
6. _____

Subs:

_____

_____

"teach me to number my days"
24 Hours

SCORE SHEET (Recap of the day)

_____
_____
_____
_____
_____
_____
_____
_____
_____
_____
_____
_____
_____
_____
_____

Go into ***All*** the world, ***Make*** disciples, ***Empowered*** from on high.

Date:_____

SCRIPTURE—What Scripture reference(s) are you reading?

_____

EMPHASIS—What did the Holy Spirit emphasize to you as you read? (If nothing, you haven't read long enough.)

_____
_____
_____
_____
_____
_____

REPENT—What do you need to turn away from so that you may DO what you read?

_____
_____
_____
_____
_____

VOLLEY—What are some ways to share what you've learned with others?

_____
_____

EXPRESS—Express your praise, your confession, your requests to the Lord.

_____
_____
_____
_____
_____
_____
_____
_____
_____
_____
_____

__Go__ into __All__ the world, __Make__ disciples, __Empowered__ from on high.

The Lineup

(What needs to be accomplished today?)

1. _____

2. _____

3. _____

4. _____

5. _____

6. _____

Subs:

_____

_____

"teach me to number my days"

24 Hours

SCORE SHEET (Recap of the day)

_____

_____

_____

_____

_____

_____

_____

_____

_____

_____

_____

_____

_____

_____

**Go** into **All** the world, **Make** disciples, **Empowered** from on high.

Date:_____

SCRIPTURE—What Scripture reference(s) are you reading?

_____

EMPHASIS—What did the Holy Spirit emphasize to you as you read? (If nothing, you haven't read long enough.)

_____
_____
_____
_____
_____
_____

REPENT—What do you need to turn away from so that you may DO what you read?

_____
_____
_____
_____
_____

VOLLEY—What are some ways to share what you've learned with others?

_____
_____

EXPRESS—Express your praise, your confession, your requests to the Lord.

_____
_____
_____
_____
_____
_____
_____
_____
_____
_____
_____
_____
_____

**Go** into **All** the world, **Make** disciples, **Empowered** from on high.

The Lineup

(What needs to be accomplished today?)

1. _____

2. _____

3. _____

4. _____

5. _____

6. _____

Subs:

_____

_____

"teach me to number my days"

24 Hours

SCORE SHEET (Recap of the day)

_____

_____

_____

_____

_____

_____

_____

_____

_____

_____

_____

_____

_____

_____

__Go__ into __All__ the world, __Make__ disciples, __Empowered__ from on high.

Date:_____

SCRIPTURE—What Scripture reference(s) are you reading?

_____

EMPHASIS—What did the Holy Spirit emphasize to you as you read? (If nothing, you haven't read long enough.)

_____
_____
_____
_____
_____
_____

REPENT—What do you need to turn away from so that you may DO what you read?

_____
_____
_____
_____
_____

VOLLEY—What are some ways to share what you've learned with others?

_____
_____

EXPRESS—Express your praise, your confession, your requests to the Lord.

_____
_____
_____
_____
_____
_____
_____
_____
_____
_____
_____
_____

_**Go**_ into _**All**_ the world, _**Make**_ disciples, _**Empowered**_ from on high.

The Lineup

(What needs to be accomplished today?)

1. _____
2. _____
3. _____
4. _____
5. _____
6. _____

Subs:

_____

_____

"teach me to number my days"

24 Hours

SCORE SHEET (Recap of the day)

**Go** into **All** the world, **Make** disciples, **Empowered** from on high.

Date:_____

SCRIPTURE—What Scripture reference(s) are you reading?

_____

EMPHASIS—What did the Holy Spirit emphasize to you as you read? (If nothing, you haven't read long enough.)

_____
_____
_____
_____
_____
_____

REPENT—What do you need to turn away from so that you may DO what you read?

_____
_____
_____
_____
_____

VOLLEY—What are some ways to share what you've learned with others?

_____
_____

EXPRESS—Express your praise, your confession, your requests to the Lord.

_____
_____
_____
_____
_____
_____
_____
_____
_____
_____
_____
_____
_____

__Go__ into __All__ the world, __Make__ disciples, __Empowered__ from on high.

The Lineup

(What needs to be accomplished today?)

1. _____
2. _____
3. _____
4. _____
5. _____
6. _____

Subs:

_____

_____

"teach me to number my days"

24 Hours

SCORE SHEET (Recap of the day)

_____

_____

_____

_____

_____

_____

_____

_____

_____

_____

_____

_____

_____

**Go** into **All** the world, **Make** disciples, **Empowered** from on high.

Date:_____

SCRIPTURE—What Scripture reference(s) are you reading?

_____

EMPHASIS—What did the Holy Spirit emphasize to you as you read? (If nothing, you haven't read long enough.)

_____
_____
_____
_____
_____
_____

REPENT—What do you need to turn away from so that you may DO what you read?

_____
_____
_____
_____
_____

VOLLEY—What are some ways to share what you've learned with others?

_____
_____

EXPRESS—Express your praise, your confession, your requests to the Lord.

_____
_____
_____
_____
_____
_____
_____
_____
_____
_____
_____
_____

__Go__ into __All__ the world, __Make__ disciples, __Empowered__ from on high.

The Lineup

(What needs to be accomplished today?)

1. _____
2. _____
3. _____
4. _____
5. _____
6. _____

Subs:

_____

_____

"teach me to number my days"

24 Hours

SCORE SHEET (Recap of the day)

_____

_____

_____

_____

_____

_____

_____

_____

_____

_____

_____

_____

_____

_____

__Go__ into __All__ the world, __Make__ disciples, __Empowered__ from on high.

Date:_____

SCRIPTURE—What Scripture reference(s) are you reading?

_____

EMPHASIS—What did the Holy Spirit emphasize to you as you read? (If nothing, you haven't read long enough.)

_____
_____
_____
_____
_____
_____

REPENT—What do you need to turn away from so that you may DO what you read?

_____
_____
_____
_____
_____

VOLLEY—What are some ways to share what you've learned with others?

_____
_____

EXPRESS—Express your praise, your confession, your requests to the Lord.

_____
_____
_____
_____
_____
_____
_____
_____
_____
_____
_____

_**Go**_ into _**All**_ the world, _**Make**_ disciples, _**Empowered**_ from on high.

The Lineup

(What needs to be accomplished today?)

1. _____
2. _____
3. _____
4. _____
5. _____
6. _____

Subs:

_____

_____

"teach me to number my days"

24 Hours

SCORE SHEET (Recap of the day)

_____
_____
_____
_____
_____
_____
_____
_____
_____
_____
_____
_____
_____
_____

**Go** into **All** the world, **Make** disciples, **Empowered** from on high.

Date:_____

SCRIPTURE—What Scripture reference(s) are you reading?

_____

EMPHASIS—What did the Holy Spirit emphasize to you as you read? (If nothing, you haven't read long enough.)

_____
_____
_____
_____
_____
_____

REPENT—What do you need to turn away from so that you may DO what you read?

_____
_____
_____
_____
_____

VOLLEY—What are some ways to share what you've learned with others?

_____
_____

EXPRESS—Express your praise, your confession, your requests to the Lord.

_____
_____
_____
_____
_____
_____
_____
_____
_____
_____
_____
_____

__Go__ into __All__ the world, __Make__ disciples, __Empowered__ from on high.

The Lineup

(What needs to be accomplished today?)

1. _____
2. _____
3. _____
4. _____
5. _____
6. _____

Subs:

_____

_____

"teach me to number my days"

24 Hours

SCORE SHEET (Recap of the day)

_____
_____
_____
_____
_____
_____
_____
_____
_____
_____
_____
_____
_____
_____

**Go** into **All** the world, **Make** disciples, **Empowered** from on high.

Date:_____

SCRIPTURE—What Scripture reference(s) are you reading?

_____

EMPHASIS—What did the Holy Spirit emphasize to you as you read? (If nothing, you haven't read long enough.)

_____
_____
_____
_____
_____
_____

REPENT—What do you need to turn away from so that you may DO what you read?

_____
_____
_____
_____
_____

VOLLEY—What are some ways to share what you've learned with others?

_____
_____

EXPRESS—Express your praise, your confession, your requests to the Lord.

_____
_____
_____
_____
_____
_____
_____
_____
_____
_____
_____
_____
_____

<u>**Go**</u> into <u>**All**</u> the world, <u>**Make**</u> disciples, <u>**Empowered**</u> from on high.

The Lineup

(What needs to be accomplished today?)

1. _____

2. _____

3. _____

4. _____

5. _____

6. _____

Subs:

_____

_____

"teach me to number my days"

24 Hours

SCORE SHEET (Recap of the day)

_____

_____

_____

_____

_____

_____

_____

_____

_____

_____

_____

_____

_____

_____

_____

Go into ***All*** the world, ***Make*** disciples, ***Empowered*** from on high.

Date:_____

SCRIPTURE—What Scripture reference(s) are you reading?

_____

EMPHASIS—What did the Holy Spirit emphasize to you as you read? (If nothing, you haven't read long enough.)

_____
_____
_____
_____
_____
_____

REPENT—What do you need to turn away from so that you may DO what you read?

_____
_____
_____
_____
_____

VOLLEY—What are some ways to share what you've learned with others?

_____
_____

EXPRESS—Express your praise, your confession, your requests to the Lord.

_____
_____
_____
_____
_____
_____
_____
_____
_____
_____
_____

*<u>Go</u> into <u>All</u> the world, <u>**Make**</u> disciples, <u>**Empowered**</u> from on high.*

The Lineup

(What needs to be accomplished today?)

1. _____
2. _____
3. _____
4. _____
5. _____
6. _____

Subs:

_____

_____

"teach me to number my days"

24 Hours

SCORE SHEET (Recap of the day)

_____
_____
_____
_____
_____
_____
_____
_____
_____
_____
_____
_____
_____
_____
_____
_____

**Go** into **All** the world, **Make** disciples, **Empowered** from on high.

Date:_____

SCRIPTURE—What Scripture reference(s) are you reading?

_____

EMPHASIS—What did the Holy Spirit emphasize to you as you read? (If nothing, you haven't read long enough.)

_____
_____
_____
_____
_____
_____

REPENT—What do you need to turn away from so that you may DO what you read?

_____
_____
_____
_____
_____

VOLLEY—What are some ways to share what you've learned with others?

_____
_____

EXPRESS—Express your praise, your confession, your requests to the Lord.

_____
_____
_____
_____
_____
_____
_____
_____
_____
_____
_____
_____
_____

_**Go**_ into _**All**_ the world, _**Make**_ disciples, _**Empowered**_ from on high.

The Lineup

(What needs to be accomplished today?)

1. _____

2. _____

3. _____

4. _____

5. _____

6. _____

Subs:

_____

_____

"teach me to number my days"

24 Hours

SCORE SHEET (Recap of the day)

_____
_____
_____
_____
_____
_____
_____
_____
_____
_____
_____
_____
_____
_____
_____

**Go** into **All** the world, **Make** disciples, **Empowered** from on high.

Date:_____

SCRIPTURE—What Scripture reference(s) are you reading?

_____

EMPHASIS—What did the Holy Spirit emphasize to you as you read? (If nothing, you haven't read long enough.)

_____
_____
_____
_____
_____
_____

REPENT—What do you need to turn away from so that you may DO what you read?

_____
_____
_____
_____
_____

VOLLEY—What are some ways to share what you've learned with others?

_____
_____

EXPRESS—Express your praise, your confession, your requests to the Lord.

_____
_____
_____
_____
_____
_____
_____
_____
_____
_____
_____

__Go__ into __All__ the world, __Make__ disciples, __Empowered__ from on high.

The Lineup

(What needs to be accomplished today?)

1. _____

2. _____

3. _____

4. _____

5. _____

6. _____

Subs:

_____

_____

"teach me to number my days"

24 Hours

SCORE SHEET (Recap of the day)

_____
_____
_____
_____
_____
_____
_____
_____
_____
_____
_____
_____
_____
_____
_____

Go into ***All*** the world, ***Make*** disciples, ***Empowered*** from on high.

Date:_____

SCRIPTURE—What Scripture reference(s) are you reading?

_____

EMPHASIS—What did the Holy Spirit emphasize to you as you read? (If nothing, you haven't read long enough.)

_____
_____
_____
_____
_____
_____

REPENT—What do you need to turn away from so that you may DO what you read?

_____
_____
_____
_____
_____

VOLLEY—What are some ways to share what you've learned with others?

_____
_____

EXPRESS—Express your praise, your confession, your requests to the Lord.

_____
_____
_____
_____
_____
_____
_____
_____
_____
_____
_____

__Go__ into __All__ the world, __Make__ disciples, __Empowered__ from on high.

The Lineup

(What needs to be accomplished today?)

1. _____
2. _____
3. _____
4. _____
5. _____
6. _____

Subs:

_____

_____

"teach me to number my days"

24 Hours

SCORE SHEET (Recap of the day)

_____
_____
_____
_____
_____
_____
_____
_____
_____
_____
_____
_____
_____
_____

_**Go**_ into _**All**_ the world, _**Make**_ disciples, _**Empowered**_ from on high.

Date:_____

S CRIPTURE—What Scripture reference(s) are you reading?

_____

E MPHASIS—What did the Holy Spirit emphasize to you as you read? (If nothing, you haven't read long enough.)

_____
_____
_____
_____
_____
_____

R EPENT—What do you need to turn away from so that you may DO what you read?

_____
_____
_____
_____
_____

V OLLEY—What are some ways to share what you've learned with others?

_____
_____

E XPRESS—Express your praise, your confession, your requests to the Lord.

_____
_____
_____
_____
_____
_____
_____
_____
_____
_____
_____
_____

__Go__ into __All__ the world, __Make__ disciples, __Empowered__ from on high.

The Lineup

(What needs to be accomplished today?)

1. _____
2. _____
3. _____
4. _____
5. _____
6. _____

Subs:

_____

_____

"teach me to number my days"

24 Hours

SCORE SHEET (Recap of the day)

_____
_____
_____
_____
_____
_____
_____
_____
_____
_____
_____
_____
_____
_____
_____
_____

Go into *All* the world, *Make* disciples, *Empowered* from on high.

Date:_____

SCRIPTURE—What Scripture reference(s) are you reading?

_____

EMPHASIS—What did the Holy Spirit emphasize to you as you read? (If nothing, you haven't read long enough.)

_____
_____
_____
_____
_____
_____

REPENT—What do you need to turn away from so that you may DO what you read?

_____
_____
_____
_____
_____

VOLLEY—What are some ways to share what you've learned with others?

_____
_____

EXPRESS—Express your praise, your confession, your requests to the Lord.

_____
_____
_____
_____
_____
_____
_____
_____
_____
_____
_____
_____

__Go__ into __All__ the world, __Make__ disciples, __Empowered__ from on high.

The Lineup

(What needs to be accomplished today?)

1. _____
2. _____
3. _____
4. _____
5. _____
6. _____

Subs:

_____

_____

"teach me to number my days" 24 Hours

SCORE SHEET (Recap of the day)

_____
_____
_____
_____
_____
_____
_____
_____
_____
_____
_____
_____
_____
_____

*<u>Go</u> into <u>All</u> the world, <u>**Make**</u> disciples, <u>**Empowered**</u> from on high.*

Date:_____

SCRIPTURE—What Scripture reference(s) are you reading?

_____

EMPHASIS—What did the Holy Spirit emphasize to you as you read? (If nothing, you haven't read long enough.)

_____
_____
_____
_____
_____
_____

REPENT—What do you need to turn away from so that you may DO what you read?

_____
_____
_____
_____
_____

VOLLEY—What are some ways to share what you've learned with others?

_____
_____

EXPRESS—Express your praise, your confession, your requests to the Lord.

_____
_____
_____
_____
_____
_____
_____
_____
_____
_____
_____
_____

_**Go**_ into _**All**_ the world, _**Make**_ disciples, _**Empowered**_ from on high.

The Lineup

(What needs to be accomplished today?)

1. _____

2. _____

3. _____

4. _____

5. _____

6. _____

Subs:

_____

_____

SCORE SHEET (Recap of the day)

_____
_____
_____
_____
_____
_____
_____
_____
_____
_____
_____
_____
_____
_____

_**Go**_ into _**All**_ the world, _**Make**_ disciples, _**Empowered**_ from on high.

Date:_____

SCRIPTURE—What Scripture reference(s) are you reading?

_____

EMPHASIS—What did the Holy Spirit emphasize to you as you read? (If nothing, you haven't read long enough.)

_____
_____
_____
_____
_____
_____

REPENT—What do you need to turn away from so that you may DO what you read?

_____
_____
_____
_____
_____

VOLLEY—What are some ways to share what you've learned with others?

_____
_____

EXPRESS—Express your praise, your confession, your requests to the Lord.

_____
_____
_____
_____
_____
_____
_____
_____
_____
_____
_____

Go into ***All*** the world, ***Make*** disciples, ***Empowered*** from on high.

The Lineup

(What needs to be accomplished today?)

1. _____

2. _____

3. _____

4. _____

5. _____

6. _____

Subs:

_____

_____

SCORE SHEET (Recap of the day)

_____
_____
_____
_____
_____
_____
_____
_____
_____
_____
_____
_____
_____
_____

__Go__ into *__All__* the world, *__Make__* disciples, *__Empowered__* from on high.

Date:_____

SCRIPTURE—What Scripture reference(s) are you reading?

_____

EMPHASIS—What did the Holy Spirit emphasize to you as you read? (If nothing, you haven't read long enough.)

_____
_____
_____
_____
_____
_____

REPENT—What do you need to turn away from so that you may DO what you read?

_____
_____
_____
_____
_____

VOLLEY—What are some ways to share what you've learned with others?

_____
_____

EXPRESS—Express your praise, your confession, your requests to the Lord.

_____
_____
_____
_____
_____
_____
_____
_____
_____
_____
_____

__Go__ into __All__ the world, __Make__ disciples, __Empowered__ from on high.

The Lineup

(What needs to be accomplished today?)

1. _____

2. _____

3. _____

4. _____

5. _____

6. _____

Subs:

_____

_____

"teach me to number my days" — 24 Hours

SCORE SHEET (Recap of the day)

_____
_____
_____
_____
_____
_____
_____
_____
_____
_____
_____
_____
_____
_____

Go into *All* the world, *Make* disciples, *Empowered* from on high.

Date:_____

SCRIPTURE—What Scripture reference(s) are you reading?

_____

EMPHASIS—What did the Holy Spirit emphasize to you as you read? (If nothing, you haven't read long enough.)

_____
_____
_____
_____
_____
_____

REPENT—What do you need to turn away from so that you may DO what you read?

_____
_____
_____
_____

VOLLEY—What are some ways to share what you've learned with others?

_____
_____

EXPRESS—Express your praise, your confession, your requests to the Lord.

_____
_____
_____
_____
_____
_____
_____
_____
_____
_____
_____

__Go__ into __All__ the world, __Make__ disciples, __Empowered__ from on high.

The Lineup

(What needs to be accomplished today?)

1. _____
2. _____
3. _____
4. _____
5. _____
6. _____

Subs:

_____

_____

"teach me to number my days"

24 Hours

SCORE SHEET (Recap of the day)

_____

_____

_____

_____

_____

_____

_____

_____

_____

_____

_____

_____

_____

_____

__Go__ into *__All__* the world, *__Make__* disciples, *__Empowered__* from on high.

Date:_____

SCRIPTURE—What Scripture reference(s) are you reading?

_____

EMPHASIS—What did the Holy Spirit emphasize to you as you read? (If nothing, you haven't read long enough.)

_____
_____
_____
_____
_____
_____

REPENT—What do you need to turn away from so that you may DO what you read?

_____
_____
_____
_____
_____

VOLLEY—What are some ways to share what you've learned with others?

_____
_____

EXPRESS—Express your praise, your confession, your requests to the Lord.

_____
_____
_____
_____
_____
_____
_____
_____
_____
_____
_____
_____

__Go__ into __All__ the world, __Make__ disciples, __Empowered__ from on high.

The Lineup

(What needs to be accomplished today?)

1. _____

2. _____

3. _____

4. _____

5. _____

6. _____

Subs:

_____

_____

SCORE SHEET (Recap of the day)

_____
_____
_____
_____
_____
_____
_____
_____
_____
_____
_____
_____
_____
_____
_____

__Go__ into __All__ the world, __Make__ disciples, __Empowered__ from on high.

Date:_____

SCRIPTURE—What Scripture reference(s) are you reading?

_____

EMPHASIS—What did the Holy Spirit emphasize to you as you read? (If nothing, you haven't read long enough.)

_____
_____
_____
_____
_____
_____

REPENT—What do you need to turn away from so that you may DO what you read?

_____
_____
_____
_____
_____

VOLLEY—What are some ways to share what you've learned with others?

_____
_____

EXPRESS—Express your praise, your confession, your requests to the Lord.

_____
_____
_____
_____
_____
_____
_____
_____
_____
_____
_____

__Go__ into __All__ the world, __Make__ disciples, __Empowered__ from on high.

The Lineup

(What needs to be accomplished today?)

1. _____

2. _____

3. _____

4. _____

5. _____

6. _____

Subs:

_____

_____

"teach me to number my days"

24 Hours

SCORE SHEET (Recap of the day)

_____

_____

_____

_____

_____

_____

_____

_____

_____

_____

_____

_____

_____

_____

_**Go**_ into _**All**_ the world, _**Make**_ disciples, _**Empowered**_ from on high.

Date:_____

SCRIPTURE—What Scripture reference(s) are you reading?

_____

EMPHASIS—What did the Holy Spirit emphasize to you as you read? (If nothing, you haven't read long enough.)

_____
_____
_____
_____
_____
_____

REPENT—What do you need to turn away from so that you may DO what you read?

_____
_____
_____
_____
_____

VOLLEY—What are some ways to share what you've learned with others?

_____
_____

EXPRESS—Express your praise, your confession, your requests to the Lord.

_____
_____
_____
_____
_____
_____
_____
_____
_____
_____
_____
_____

__Go__ into __All__ the world, __Make__ disciples, __Empowered__ from on high.

The Lineup

(What needs to be accomplished today?)

1. _____

2. _____

3. _____

4. _____

5. _____

6. _____

Subs:

_____

_____

"teach me to number my days"

24 Hours

SCORE SHEET (Recap of the day)

_____
_____
_____
_____
_____
_____
_____
_____
_____
_____
_____
_____
_____
_____
_____

_**Go**_ into _**All**_ the world, _**Make**_ disciples, _**Empowered**_ from on high.

Date:_____

Sᴄʀɪᴘᴛᴜʀᴇ—What Scripture reference(s) are you reading?

_____

Eᴍᴘʜᴀsɪs—What did the Holy Spirit emphasize to you as you read? (If nothing, you haven't read long enough.)

_____
_____
_____
_____
_____
_____

Rᴇᴘᴇɴᴛ—What do you need to turn away from so that you may DO what you read?

_____
_____
_____
_____
_____

Vᴏʟʟᴇʏ—What are some ways to share what you've learned with others?

_____
_____

Exᴘʀᴇss—Express your praise, your confession, your requests to the Lord.

_____
_____
_____
_____
_____
_____
_____
_____
_____
_____
_____

__Go__ into __All__ the world, __Make__ disciples, __Empowered__ from on high.

The Lineup

(What needs to be accomplished today?)

1. _____

2. _____

3. _____

4. _____

5. _____

6. _____

Subs:

_____

_____

"teach me to number my days"

24 Hours

SCORE SHEET (Recap of the day)

_____
_____
_____
_____
_____
_____
_____
_____
_____
_____
_____
_____
_____
_____
_____
_____
_____

***Go** into **All** the world, **Make** disciples, **Empowered** from on high.*

Date:_____

SCRIPTURE—What Scripture reference(s) are you reading?

_____

EMPHASIS—What did the Holy Spirit emphasize to you as you read? (If nothing, you haven't read long enough.)

_____
_____
_____
_____
_____
_____

REPENT—What do you need to turn away from so that you may DO what you read?

_____
_____
_____
_____
_____

VOLLEY—What are some ways to share what you've learned with others?

_____
_____

EXPRESS—Express your praise, your confession, your requests to the Lord.

_____
_____
_____
_____
_____
_____
_____
_____
_____
_____
_____
_____

_**Go**_ into _**All**_ the world, _**Make**_ disciples, _**Empowered**_ from on high.

The Lineup

(What needs to be accomplished today?)

1. _____
2. _____
3. _____
4. _____
5. _____
6. _____

Subs:

_____

_____

"teach me to number my days"

24 Hours

SCORE SHEET (Recap of the day)

_____
_____
_____
_____
_____
_____
_____
_____
_____
_____
_____
_____
_____
_____

__Go__ into __All__ the world, __Make__ disciples, __Empowered__ from on high.

Date:_____

S CRIPTURE—What Scripture reference(s) are you reading?

_____

E MPHASIS—What did the Holy Spirit emphasize to you as you read? (If nothing, you haven't read long enough.)

_____
_____
_____
_____
_____
_____

R EPENT—What do you need to turn away from so that you may DO what you read?

_____
_____
_____
_____
_____

V OLLEY—What are some ways to share what you've learned with others?

_____
_____

E XPRESS—Express your praise, your confession, your requests to the Lord.

_____
_____
_____
_____
_____
_____
_____
_____
_____
_____
_____
_____

__Go__ into __All__ the world, __Make__ disciples, __Empowered__ from on high.

The Lineup

(What needs to be accomplished today?)

1. _____

2. _____

3. _____

4. _____

5. _____

6. _____

Subs:

_____

_____

"teach me to number my days"

24 Hours

SCORE SHEET (Recap of the day)

_____

_____

_____

_____

_____

_____

_____

_____

_____

_____

_____

_____

_____

_____

_____

__Go__ into __All__ the world, __Make__ disciples, __Empowered__ from on high.

Date:_____

SCRIPTURE—What Scripture reference(s) are you reading?

_____

EMPHASIS—What did the Holy Spirit emphasize to you as you read? (If nothing, you haven't read long enough.)

_____
_____
_____
_____
_____
_____

REPENT—What do you need to turn away from so that you may DO what you read?

_____
_____
_____
_____
_____

VOLLEY—What are some ways to share what you've learned with others?

_____
_____

EXPRESS—Express your praise, your confession, your requests to the Lord.

_____
_____
_____
_____
_____
_____
_____
_____
_____
_____
_____
_____

***Go** into **All** the world, **Make** disciples, **Empowered** from on high.*

The Lineup

(What needs to be accomplished today?)

1. _____
2. _____
3. _____
4. _____
5. _____
6. _____

Subs:

_____

_____

"teach me to number my days"

24 Hours

SCORE SHEET (Recap of the day)

_____
_____
_____
_____
_____
_____
_____
_____
_____
_____
_____
_____
_____
_____
_____

**Go** into **All** the world, **Make** disciples, **Empowered** from on high.

Date:_____

SCRIPTURE—What Scripture reference(s) are you reading?

_____

EMPHASIS—What did the Holy Spirit emphasize to you as you read? (If nothing, you haven't read long enough.)

_____
_____
_____
_____
_____
_____

REPENT—What do you need to turn away from so that you may DO what you read?

_____
_____
_____
_____
_____

VOLLEY—What are some ways to share what you've learned with others?

_____
_____

EXPRESS—Express your praise, your confession, your requests to the Lord.

_____
_____
_____
_____
_____
_____
_____
_____
_____
_____
_____

__Go__ into __All__ the world, __Make__ disciples, __Empowered__ from on high.

The Lineup

(What needs to be accomplished today?)

1. _____

2. _____

3. _____

4. _____

5. _____

6. _____

Subs:

_____

_____

"teach me to number my days"

24 Hours

SCORE SHEET (Recap of the day)

_____

_____

_____

_____

_____

_____

_____

_____

_____

_____

_____

_____

_____

_____

**Go** into **All** the world, **Make** disciples, **Empowered** from on high.

Date:_____

SCRIPTURE—What Scripture reference(s) are you reading?

_____

EMPHASIS—What did the Holy Spirit emphasize to you as you read? (If nothing, you haven't read long enough.)

_____
_____
_____
_____
_____
_____

REPENT—What do you need to turn away from so that you may DO what you read?

_____
_____
_____
_____
_____

VOLLEY—What are some ways to share what you've learned with others?

_____
_____

EXPRESS—Express your praise, your confession, your requests to the Lord.

_____
_____
_____
_____
_____
_____
_____
_____
_____
_____
_____
_____

***Go** into **All** the world, **Make** disciples, **Empowered** from on high.*

The Lineup

(What needs to be accomplished today?)

1. _____

2. _____

3. _____

4. _____

5. _____

6. _____

Subs:

_____

_____

"teach me to number my days"

24 Hours

SCORE SHEET (Recap of the day)

_____

_____

_____

_____

_____

_____

_____

_____

_____

_____

_____

_____

_____

_____

__Go__ into __All__ the world, __Make__ disciples, __Empowered__ from on high.

Date:_____

SCRIPTURE—What Scripture reference(s) are you reading?

_____

EMPHASIS—What did the Holy Spirit emphasize to you as you read? (If nothing, you haven't read long enough.)

_____
_____
_____
_____
_____
_____

REPENT—What do you need to turn away from so that you may DO what you read?

_____
_____
_____
_____
_____

VOLLEY—What are some ways to share what you've learned with others?

_____
_____

EXPRESS—Express your praise, your confession, your requests to the Lord.

_____
_____
_____
_____
_____
_____
_____
_____
_____
_____
_____
_____

_**Go**_ into _**All**_ the world, _**Make**_ disciples, _**Empowered**_ from on high.

The Lineup

(What needs to be accomplished today?)

1. _____

2. _____

3. _____

4. _____

5. _____

6. _____

Subs:

_____

_____

"teach me to number my days"

24 Hours

SCORE SHEET (Recap of the day)

_____
_____
_____
_____
_____
_____
_____
_____
_____
_____
_____
_____
_____
_____
_____

**Go** into **All** the world, **Make** disciples, **Empowered** from on high.

Date:_____

SCRIPTURE—What Scripture reference(s) are you reading?

_____

EMPHASIS—What did the Holy Spirit emphasize to you as you read? (If nothing, you haven't read long enough.)

_____
_____
_____
_____
_____
_____

REPENT—What do you need to turn away from so that you may DO what you read?

_____
_____
_____
_____
_____

VOLLEY—What are some ways to share what you've learned with others?

_____
_____

EXPRESS—Express your praise, your confession, your requests to the Lord.

_____
_____
_____
_____
_____
_____
_____
_____
_____
_____
_____

__Go__ into __All__ the world, __Make__ disciples, __Empowered__ from on high.

The Lineup

(What needs to be accomplished today?)

1. _____

2. _____

3. _____

4. _____

5. _____

6. _____

Subs:

_____

_____

"teach me to number my days"

24 Hours

SCORE SHEET (Recap of the day)

_____
_____
_____
_____
_____
_____
_____
_____
_____
_____
_____
_____
_____
_____

_Go_ into **_All_** the world, **_Make_** disciples, **_Empowered_** from on high.

Date:_____

SCRIPTURE—What Scripture reference(s) are you reading?

_____

EMPHASIS—What did the Holy Spirit emphasize to you as you read? (If nothing, you haven't read long enough.)

_____
_____
_____
_____
_____
_____

REPENT—What do you need to turn away from so that you may DO what you read?

_____
_____
_____
_____
_____

VOLLEY—What are some ways to share what you've learned with others?

_____
_____

EXPRESS—Express your praise, your confession, your requests to the Lord.

_____
_____
_____
_____
_____
_____
_____
_____
_____
_____
_____
_____

__Go__ into __All__ the world, __Make__ disciples, __Empowered__ from on high.

The Lineup

(What needs to be accomplished today?)

1. _____

2. _____

3. _____

4. _____

5. _____

6. _____

Subs:

_____

_____

"teach me to number my days"

24 Hours

SCORE SHEET (Recap of the day)

_____
_____
_____
_____
_____
_____
_____
_____
_____
_____
_____
_____
_____
_____
_____

__Go__ into __All__ the world, __Make__ disciples, __Empowered__ from on high.

Date:_____

SCRIPTURE—What Scripture reference(s) are you reading?

_____

EMPHASIS—What did the Holy Spirit emphasize to you as you read? (If nothing, you haven't read long enough.)

_____
_____
_____
_____
_____
_____

REPENT—What do you need to turn away from so that you may DO what you read?

_____
_____
_____
_____
_____

VOLLEY—What are some ways to share what you've learned with others?

_____
_____

EXPRESS—Express your praise, your confession, your requests to the Lord.

_____
_____
_____
_____
_____
_____
_____
_____
_____
_____
_____
_____

__Go__ into __All__ the world, __Make__ disciples, __Empowered__ from on high.

The Lineup

(What needs to be accomplished today?)

1. _____

2. _____

3. _____

4. _____

5. _____

6. _____

Subs:

_____

_____

"teach me to number my days"

24 Hours

SCORE SHEET (Recap of the day)

_____

_____

_____

_____

_____

_____

_____

_____

_____

_____

_____

_____

_____

_____

__Go__ into __All__ the world, __Make__ disciples, __Empowered__ from on high.

Date:_____

Sᴄʀɪᴘᴛᴜʀᴇ—What Scripture reference(s) are you reading?

_____

Eᴍᴘʜᴀsɪs—What did the Holy Spirit emphasize to you as you read? (If nothing, you haven't read long enough.)

_____
_____
_____
_____
_____
_____

Rᴇᴘᴇɴᴛ—What do you need to turn away from so that you may DO what you read?

_____
_____
_____
_____
_____

Vᴏʟʟᴇʏ—What are some ways to share what you've learned with others?

_____
_____

Exᴘʀᴇss—Express your praise, your confession, your requests to the Lord.

_____
_____
_____
_____
_____
_____
_____
_____
_____
_____
_____
_____
_____

__Go__ into __All__ the world, __Make__ disciples, __Empowered__ from on high.

The Lineup

(What needs to be accomplished today?)

1. _____

2. _____

3. _____

4. _____

5. _____

6. _____

Subs:

_____

_____

"teach me to number my days"

24 Hours

SCORE SHEET (Recap of the day)

_____
_____
_____
_____
_____
_____
_____
_____
_____
_____
_____
_____
_____
_____
_____
_____

__Go__ into __All__ the world, __Make__ disciples, __Empowered__ from on high.

Date:_____

SCRIPTURE—What Scripture reference(s) are you reading?

_____

EMPHASIS—What did the Holy Spirit emphasize to you as you read? (If nothing, you haven't read long enough.)

_____
_____
_____
_____
_____
_____

REPENT—What do you need to turn away from so that you may DO what you read?

_____
_____
_____
_____
_____

VOLLEY—What are some ways to share what you've learned with others?

_____
_____

EXPRESS—Express your praise, your confession, your requests to the Lord.

_____
_____
_____
_____
_____
_____
_____
_____
_____
_____
_____

__Go__ into __All__ the world, __Make__ disciples, __Empowered__ from on high.

The Lineup

(What needs to be accomplished today?)

1. _____

2. _____

3. _____

4. _____

5. _____

6. _____

Subs:

_____

_____

SCORE SHEET (Recap of the day)

_____
_____
_____
_____
_____
_____
_____
_____
_____
_____
_____
_____
_____
_____

"teach me to number my days"

24 Hours

_**Go**_ into _**All**_ the world, _**Make**_ disciples, _**Empowered**_ from on high.

Date:_____

SCRIPTURE—What Scripture reference(s) are you reading?

_____

EMPHASIS—What did the Holy Spirit emphasize to you as you read? (If nothing, you haven't read long enough.)

_____
_____
_____
_____
_____
_____

REPENT—What do you need to turn away from so that you may DO what you read?

_____
_____
_____
_____
_____

VOLLEY—What are some ways to share what you've learned with others?

_____
_____

EXPRESS—Express your praise, your confession, your requests to the Lord.

_____
_____
_____
_____
_____
_____
_____
_____
_____
_____
_____
_____

__Go__ into __All__ the world, __Make__ disciples, __Empowered__ from on high.

The Lineup

(What needs to be accomplished today?)

1. _____

2. _____

3. _____

4. _____

5. _____

6. _____

Subs:

_____

_____

SCORE SHEET (Recap of the day)

_____
_____
_____
_____
_____
_____
_____
_____
_____
_____
_____
_____
_____
_____

__Go__ into __All__ the world, __Make__ disciples, __Empowered__ from on high.

Date:_____

SCRIPTURE—What Scripture reference(s) are you reading?

_____

EMPHASIS—What did the Holy Spirit emphasize to you as you read? (If nothing, you haven't read long enough.)

_____
_____
_____
_____
_____
_____

REPENT—What do you need to turn away from so that you may DO what you read?

_____
_____
_____
_____
_____

VOLLEY—What are some ways to share what you've learned with others?

_____
_____

EXPRESS—Express your praise, your confession, your requests to the Lord.

_____
_____
_____
_____
_____
_____
_____
_____
_____
_____
_____

**Go** into **All** the world, **Make** disciples, **Empowered** from on high.

The Lineup

(What needs to be accomplished today?)

1. _____

2. _____

3. _____

4. _____

5. _____

6. _____

Subs:

_____

_____

"teach me to number my days"

24 Hours

SCORE SHEET (Recap of the day)

_____
_____
_____
_____
_____
_____
_____
_____
_____
_____
_____
_____
_____
_____
_____
_____

_Go_ into _All_ the world, _Make_ disciples, _Empowered_ from on high.

Date:_____

SCRIPTURE—What Scripture reference(s) are you reading?

_____

EMPHASIS—What did the Holy Spirit emphasize to you as you read? (If nothing, you haven't read long enough.)

_____
_____
_____
_____
_____
_____

REPENT—What do you need to turn away from so that you may DO what you read?

_____
_____
_____
_____
_____

VOLLEY—What are some ways to share what you've learned with others?

_____
_____

EXPRESS—Express your praise, your confession, your requests to the Lord.

_____
_____
_____
_____
_____
_____
_____
_____
_____
_____
_____
_____

__Go__ into __All__ the world, __Make__ disciples, __Empowered__ from on high.

The Lineup

(What needs to be accomplished today?)

1. _____

2. _____

3. _____

4. _____

5. _____

6. _____

Subs:

_____

_____

"teach me to number my days"

24 Hours

SCORE SHEET (Recap of the day)

_____

_____

_____

_____

_____

_____

_____

_____

_____

_____

_____

_____

_____

__Go__ into __All__ the world, __Make__ disciples, __Empowered__ from on high.

Date:_____

SCRIPTURE—What Scripture reference(s) are you reading?

_____

EMPHASIS—What did the Holy Spirit emphasize to you as you read? (If nothing, you haven't read long enough.)

_____
_____
_____
_____
_____
_____

REPENT—What do you need to turn away from so that you may DO what you read?

_____
_____
_____
_____
_____

VOLLEY—What are some ways to share what you've learned with others?

_____
_____

EXPRESS—Express your praise, your confession, your requests to the Lord.

_____
_____
_____
_____
_____
_____
_____
_____
_____
_____
_____

__Go__ into __All__ the world, __Make__ disciples, __Empowered__ from on high.

The Lineup

(What needs to be accomplished today?)

1. _____
2. _____
3. _____
4. _____
5. _____
6. _____

Subs:

_____

_____

SCORE SHEET (Recap of the day)

_____
_____
_____
_____
_____
_____
_____
_____
_____
_____
_____
_____
_____
_____
_____

__Go__ into __All__ the world, __Make__ disciples, __Empowered__ from on high.

Date:_____

SCRIPTURE—What Scripture reference(s) are you reading?

_____

EMPHASIS—What did the Holy Spirit emphasize to you as you read? (If nothing, you haven't read long enough.)

_____
_____
_____
_____
_____
_____

REPENT—What do you need to turn away from so that you may DO what you read?

_____
_____
_____
_____
_____

VOLLEY—What are some ways to share what you've learned with others?

_____
_____

EXPRESS—Express your praise, your confession, your requests to the Lord.

_____
_____
_____
_____
_____
_____
_____
_____
_____
_____
_____
_____

__Go__ into __All__ the world, __Make__ disciples, __Empowered__ from on high.

The Lineup

(What needs to be accomplished today?)

1. _____
2. _____
3. _____
4. _____
5. _____
6. _____

Subs:

_____

_____

"teach me to number my days"

24 Hours

SCORE SHEET (Recap of the day)

_____
_____
_____
_____
_____
_____
_____
_____
_____
_____
_____
_____
_____
_____
_____

__Go__ into __All__ the world, __Make__ disciples, __Empowered__ from on high.

Date:_____

Sᴄʀɪᴘᴛᴜʀᴇ—What Scripture reference(s) are you reading?

_____

Eᴍᴘʜᴀsɪs—What did the Holy Spirit emphasize to you as you read? (If nothing, you haven't read long enough.)

_____
_____
_____
_____
_____
_____

Rᴇᴘᴇɴᴛ—What do you need to turn away from so that you may DO what you read?

_____
_____
_____
_____
_____

Vᴏʟʟᴇʏ—What are some ways to share what you've learned with others?

_____
_____

Exᴘʀᴇss—Express your praise, your confession, your requests to the Lord.

_____
_____
_____
_____
_____
_____
_____
_____
_____
_____
_____
_____

__Go__ into __All__ the world, __Make__ disciples, __Empowered__ from on high.

The Lineup

(What needs to be accomplished today?)

1. _____

2. _____

3. _____

4. _____

5. _____

6. _____

Subs:

_____

_____

"teach me to number my days"

24 Hours

SCORE SHEET (Recap of the day)

_____
_____
_____
_____
_____
_____
_____
_____
_____
_____
_____
_____
_____
_____

__Go__ into __All__ the world, __Make__ disciples, __Empowered__ from on high.

Date:_____

Sᴄʀɪᴘᴛᴜʀᴇ—What Scripture reference(s) are you reading?

_____

Eᴍᴘʜᴀsɪs—What did the Holy Spirit emphasize to you as you read? (If nothing, you haven't read long enough.)

_____
_____
_____
_____
_____
_____

Rᴇᴘᴇɴᴛ—What do you need to turn away from so that you may DO what you read?

_____
_____
_____
_____
_____

Vᴏʟʟᴇʏ—What are some ways to share what you've learned with others?

_____
_____

Exᴘʀᴇss—Express your praise, your confession, your requests to the Lord.

_____
_____
_____
_____
_____
_____
_____
_____
_____
_____
_____

_**Go**_ into _**All**_ the world, _**Make**_ disciples, _**Empowered**_ from on high.

The Lineup

(What needs to be accomplished today?)

1. _____

2. _____

3. _____

4. _____

5. _____

6. _____

Subs:

_____

_____

"teach me to number my days"

24 Hours

SCORE SHEET (Recap of the day)

_____
_____
_____
_____
_____
_____
_____
_____
_____
_____
_____
_____
_____
_____

__Go__ into __All__ the world, __Make__ disciples, __Empowered__ from on high.

Date:_____

SCRIPTURE—What Scripture reference(s) are you reading?

_____

EMPHASIS—What did the Holy Spirit emphasize to you as you read? (If nothing, you haven't read long enough.)

_____
_____
_____
_____
_____
_____

REPENT—What do you need to turn away from so that you may DO what you read?

_____
_____
_____
_____
_____

VOLLEY—What are some ways to share what you've learned with others?

_____
_____

EXPRESS—Express your praise, your confession, your requests to the Lord.

_____
_____
_____
_____
_____
_____
_____
_____
_____
_____
_____
_____
_____
_____

__Go__ into __All__ the world, __Make__ disciples, __Empowered__ from on high.

The Lineup

(What needs to be accomplished today?)

1. _____

2. _____

3. _____

4. _____

5. _____

6. _____

Subs:

_____

_____

"teach me to number my days"

24 Hours

SCORE SHEET (Recap of the day)

_____
_____
_____
_____
_____
_____
_____
_____
_____
_____
_____
_____
_____
_____

__Go__ into __All__ the world, __Make__ disciples, __Empowered__ from on high.

Date:_____

SCRIPTURE—What Scripture reference(s) are you reading?

_____

EMPHASIS—What did the Holy Spirit emphasize to you as you read? (If nothing, you haven't read long enough.)

_____
_____
_____
_____
_____
_____

REPENT—What do you need to turn away from so that you may DO what you read?

_____
_____
_____
_____
_____

VOLLEY—What are some ways to share what you've learned with others?

_____
_____

EXPRESS—Express your praise, your confession, your requests to the Lord.

_____
_____
_____
_____
_____
_____
_____
_____
_____
_____

_**Go**_ into _**All**_ the world, _**Make**_ disciples, _**Empowered**_ from on high.

The Lineup

(What needs to be accomplished today?)

1. _____
2. _____
3. _____
4. _____
5. _____
6. _____

Subs:

_____

_____

"teach me to number my days"

24 Hours

SCORE SHEET (Recap of the day)

_____
_____
_____
_____
_____
_____
_____
_____
_____
_____
_____
_____
_____
_____

Go into ***All*** the world, ***Make*** disciples, ***Empowered*** from on high.

Date:_____

SCRIPTURE—What Scripture reference(s) are you reading?

_____

EMPHASIS—What did the Holy Spirit emphasize to you as you read? (If nothing, you haven't read long enough.)

_____
_____
_____
_____
_____
_____

REPENT—What do you need to turn away from so that you may DO what you read?

_____
_____
_____
_____
_____

VOLLEY—What are some ways to share what you've learned with others?

_____
_____

EXPRESS—Express your praise, your confession, your requests to the Lord.

_____
_____
_____
_____
_____
_____
_____
_____
_____
_____
_____
_____
_____
_____

***Go** into **All** the world, **Make** disciples, **Empowered** from on high.*

The Lineup

(What needs to be accomplished today?)

1. _____

2. _____

3. _____

4. _____

5. _____

6. _____

Subs:

_____

_____

"teach me to number my days"

24 Hours

SCORE SHEET (Recap of the day)

_____
_____
_____
_____
_____
_____
_____
_____
_____
_____
_____
_____
_____
_____
_____

__Go__ into __All__ the world, __Make__ disciples, __Empowered__ from on high.

Date:_____

SCRIPTURE—What Scripture reference(s) are you reading?

_____

EMPHASIS—What did the Holy Spirit emphasize to you as you read? (If nothing, you haven't read long enough.)

_____
_____
_____
_____
_____
_____

REPENT—What do you need to turn away from so that you may DO what you read?

_____
_____
_____
_____
_____

VOLLEY—What are some ways to share what you've learned with others?

_____
_____

EXPRESS—Express your praise, your confession, your requests to the Lord.

_____
_____
_____
_____
_____
_____
_____
_____
_____
_____
_____

**Go** into **All** the world, **Make** disciples, **Empowered** from on high.

The Lineup

(What needs to be accomplished today?)

1. _____

2. _____

3. _____

4. _____

5. _____

6. _____

Subs:

_____

_____

"teach me to number my days"

24 Hours

SCORE SHEET (Recap of the day)

_____
_____
_____
_____
_____
_____
_____
_____
_____
_____
_____
_____
_____
_____

*__Go__ into __All__ the world, **Make** disciples, **Empowered** from on high.*

Date:_____

Sᴄʀɪᴘᴛᴜʀᴇ—What Scripture reference(s) are you reading?

_____

Eᴍᴘʜᴀsɪs—What did the Holy Spirit emphasize to you as you read? (If nothing, you haven't read long enough.)

_____
_____
_____
_____
_____
_____

Rᴇᴘᴇɴᴛ—What do you need to turn away from so that you may DO what you read?

_____
_____
_____
_____
_____

Vᴏʟʟᴇʏ—What are some ways to share what you've learned with others?

_____
_____

Eхᴘʀᴇss—Express your praise, your confession, your requests to the Lord.

_____
_____
_____
_____
_____
_____
_____
_____
_____
_____
_____

__Go__ into __All__ the world, __Make__ disciples, __Empowered__ from on high.

The Lineup

(What needs to be accomplished today?)

1. _____

2. _____

3. _____

4. _____

5. _____

6. _____

Subs:

_____

_____

"teach me to number my days"

24 Hours

SCORE SHEET (Recap of the day)

_____
_____
_____
_____
_____
_____
_____
_____
_____
_____
_____
_____
_____
_____

**Go** into **All** the world, **Make** disciples, **Empowered** from on high.

Date:_____

SCRIPTURE—What Scripture reference(s) are you reading?

_____

EMPHASIS—What did the Holy Spirit emphasize to you as you read? (If nothing, you haven't read long enough.)

_____
_____
_____
_____
_____
_____

REPENT—What do you need to turn away from so that you may DO what you read?

_____
_____
_____
_____
_____

VOLLEY—What are some ways to share what you've learned with others?

_____
_____

EXPRESS—Express your praise, your confession, your requests to the Lord.

_____
_____
_____
_____
_____
_____
_____
_____
_____
_____
_____
_____
_____

__Go__ into __All__ the world, __Make__ disciples, __Empowered__ from on high.

The Lineup

(What needs to be accomplished today?)

1. _____
2. _____
3. _____
4. _____
5. _____
6. _____

Subs:

_____

_____

"teach me to number my days"

24 Hours

SCORE SHEET (Recap of the day)

_____
_____
_____
_____
_____
_____
_____
_____
_____
_____
_____
_____
_____
_____
_____

**Go** into **All** the world, **Make** disciples, **Empowered** from on high.

Date:_____

SCRIPTURE—What Scripture reference(s) are you reading?

_____

EMPHASIS—What did the Holy Spirit emphasize to you as you read? (If nothing, you haven't read long enough.)

_____
_____
_____
_____
_____
_____

REPENT—What do you need to turn away from so that you may DO what you read?

_____
_____
_____
_____
_____

VOLLEY—What are some ways to share what you've learned with others?

_____
_____

EXPRESS—Express your praise, your confession, your requests to the Lord.

_____
_____
_____
_____
_____
_____
_____
_____
_____
_____
_____
_____

__Go__ into __All__ the world, __Make__ disciples, __Empowered__ from on high.

The Lineup

(What needs to be accomplished today?)

1. _____

2. _____

3. _____

4. _____

5. _____

6. _____

Subs:

_____

_____

"teach me to number my days"

24 Hours

SCORE SHEET (Recap of the day)

_____
_____
_____
_____
_____
_____
_____
_____
_____
_____
_____
_____
_____
_____

__Go__ into __All__ the world, __Make__ disciples, __Empowered__ from on high.

Date:_____

SCRIPTURE—What Scripture reference(s) are you reading?

_____

EMPHASIS—What did the Holy Spirit emphasize to you as you read? (If nothing, you haven't read long enough.)

_____
_____
_____
_____
_____
_____

REPENT—What do you need to turn away from so that you may DO what you read?

_____
_____
_____
_____
_____

VOLLEY—What are some ways to share what you've learned with others?

_____
_____

EXPRESS—Express your praise, your confession, your requests to the Lord.

_____
_____
_____
_____
_____
_____
_____
_____
_____
_____
_____
_____

__Go__ into __All__ the world, __Make__ disciples, __Empowered__ from on high.

The Lineup

(What needs to be accomplished today?)

1. _____

2. _____

3. _____

4. _____

5. _____

6. _____

Subs:

_____

_____

"teach me to number my days"

24 Hours

SCORE SHEET (Recap of the day)

_____
_____
_____
_____
_____
_____
_____
_____
_____
_____
_____
_____
_____
_____
_____

__Go__ into __All__ the world, __Make__ disciples, __Empowered__ from on high.

Date:_____

SCRIPTURE—What Scripture reference(s) are you reading?

_____

EMPHASIS—What did the Holy Spirit emphasize to you as you read? (If nothing, you haven't read long enough.)

_____
_____
_____
_____
_____
_____

REPENT—What do you need to turn away from so that you may DO what you read?

_____
_____
_____
_____
_____

VOLLEY—What are some ways to share what you've learned with others?

_____
_____

EXPRESS—Express your praise, your confession, your requests to the Lord.

_____
_____
_____
_____
_____
_____
_____
_____
_____
_____
_____

_**Go**_ into _**All**_ the world, _**Make**_ disciples, _**Empowered**_ from on high.

The Lineup

(What needs to be accomplished today?)

1. _____

2. _____

3. _____

4. _____

5. _____

6. _____

Subs:

_____

_____

SCORE SHEET (Recap of the day)

_____
_____
_____
_____
_____
_____
_____
_____
_____
_____
_____
_____
_____
_____
_____
_____

__Go__ into *__All__* the world, *__Make__* disciples, *__Empowered__* from on high.

Date:_____

SCRIPTURE—What Scripture reference(s) are you reading?

_____

EMPHASIS—What did the Holy Spirit emphasize to you as you read? (If nothing, you haven't read long enough.)

_____
_____
_____
_____
_____
_____

REPENT—What do you need to turn away from so that you may DO what you read?

_____
_____
_____
_____
_____

VOLLEY—What are some ways to share what you've learned with others?

_____
_____

EXPRESS—Express your praise, your confession, your requests to the Lord.

_____
_____
_____
_____
_____
_____
_____
_____
_____
_____
_____
_____

__Go__ into __All__ the world, __Make__ disciples, __Empowered__ from on high.

The Lineup

(What needs to be accomplished today?)

1. _____
2. _____
3. _____
4. _____
5. _____
6. _____

Subs:

_____

_____

"teach me to number my days"

24 Hours

SCORE SHEET (Recap of the day)

_____
_____
_____
_____
_____
_____
_____
_____
_____
_____
_____
_____
_____
_____
_____
_____

_Go_ into _All_ the world, _Make_ disciples, _Empowered_ from on high.

Date:_____

SCRIPTURE—What Scripture reference(s) are you reading?

_____

EMPHASIS—What did the Holy Spirit emphasize to you as you read? (If nothing, you haven't read long enough.)

_____
_____
_____
_____
_____
_____

REPENT—What do you need to turn away from so that you may DO what you read?

_____
_____
_____
_____
_____

VOLLEY—What are some ways to share what you've learned with others?

_____
_____

EXPRESS—Express your praise, your confession, your requests to the Lord.

_____
_____
_____
_____
_____
_____
_____
_____
_____
_____
_____
_____

__Go__ into __All__ the world, __Make__ disciples, __Empowered__ from on high.

The Lineup

(What needs to be accomplished today?)

1. _____
2. _____
3. _____
4. _____
5. _____
6. _____

Subs:

_____

_____

"teach me to number my days"

24 Hours

SCORE SHEET (Recap of the day)

_____
_____
_____
_____
_____
_____
_____
_____
_____
_____
_____
_____
_____
_____
_____

__Go__ into __All__ the world, __Make__ disciples, __Empowered__ from on high.

Date:_____

SCRIPTURE—What Scripture reference(s) are you reading?

_____

EMPHASIS—What did the Holy Spirit emphasize to you as you read? (If nothing, you haven't read long enough.)

_____
_____
_____
_____
_____
_____

REPENT—What do you need to turn away from so that you may DO what you read?

_____
_____
_____
_____
_____

VOLLEY—What are some ways to share what you've learned with others?

_____
_____

EXPRESS—Express your praise, your confession, your requests to the Lord.

_____
_____
_____
_____
_____
_____
_____
_____
_____
_____
_____
_____

_**Go**_ into _**All**_ the world, _**Make**_ disciples, _**Empowered**_ from on high.

The Lineup

(What needs to be accomplished today?)

1. _____

2. _____

3. _____

4. _____

5. _____

6. _____

Subs:

_____

_____

SCORE SHEET (Recap of the day)

_____
_____
_____
_____
_____
_____
_____
_____
_____
_____
_____
_____
_____
_____
_____
_____

**Go** into **All** the world, **Make** disciples, **Empowered** from on high.

Date:_____

SCRIPTURE—What Scripture reference(s) are you reading?

_____

EMPHASIS—What did the Holy Spirit emphasize to you as you read? (If nothing, you haven't read long enough.)

_____
_____
_____
_____
_____
_____

REPENT—What do you need to turn away from so that you may DO what you read?

_____
_____
_____
_____
_____

VOLLEY—What are some ways to share what you've learned with others?

_____
_____
_____

EXPRESS—Express your praise, your confession, your requests to the Lord.

_____
_____
_____
_____
_____
_____
_____
_____
_____
_____
_____
_____
_____

__Go__ into __All__ the world, __Make__ disciples, __Empowered__ from on high.

The Lineup

(What needs to be accomplished today?)

1. _____
2. _____
3. _____
4. _____
5. _____
6. _____

Subs:

_____

_____

"teach me to number my days"

24 Hours

SCORE SHEET (Recap of the day)

_____
_____
_____
_____
_____
_____
_____
_____
_____
_____
_____
_____

Go into ***All*** the world, ***Make*** disciples, ***Empowered*** from on high.

Date:_____

SCRIPTURE—What Scripture reference(s) are you reading?

_____

EMPHASIS—What did the Holy Spirit emphasize to you as you read? (If nothing, you haven't read long enough.)

_____
_____
_____
_____
_____
_____

REPENT—What do you need to turn away from so that you may DO what you read?

_____
_____
_____
_____
_____

VOLLEY—What are some ways to share what you've learned with others?

_____
_____

EXPRESS—Express your praise, your confession, your requests to the Lord.

_____
_____
_____
_____
_____
_____
_____
_____
_____
_____
_____
_____

__Go__ into __All__ the world, __Make__ disciples, __Empowered__ from on high.

The Lineup

(What needs to be accomplished today?)

1. _____

2. _____

3. _____

4. _____

5. _____

6. _____

Subs:

_____

_____

"teach me to number my days"

24 Hours

SCORE SHEET (Recap of the day)

_____
_____
_____
_____
_____
_____
_____
_____
_____
_____
_____
_____
_____
_____

__Go__ into __All__ the world, __Make__ disciples, __Empowered__ from on high.

Date:_____

SCRIPTURE—What Scripture reference(s) are you reading?

_____

EMPHASIS—What did the Holy Spirit emphasize to you as you read? (If nothing, you haven't read long enough.)

_____
_____
_____
_____
_____
_____

REPENT—What do you need to turn away from so that you may DO what you read?

_____
_____
_____
_____
_____

VOLLEY—What are some ways to share what you've learned with others?

_____
_____

EXPRESS—Express your praise, your confession, your requests to the Lord.

_____
_____
_____
_____
_____
_____
_____
_____
_____
_____
_____
_____

_Go_ into **_All_** the world, **_Make_** disciples, **_Empowered_** from on high.

The Lineup

(What needs to be accomplished today?)

1. _____

2. _____

3. _____

4. _____

5. _____

6. _____

Subs:

_____

_____

"teach me to number my days"

24 Hours

SCORE SHEET (Recap of the day)

_____
_____
_____
_____
_____
_____
_____
_____
_____
_____
_____
_____
_____
_____
_____

__Go__ into __All__ the world, __Make__ disciples, __Empowered__ from on high.

Date:_____

Sᴄʀɪᴘᴛᴜʀᴇ—What Scripture reference(s) are you reading?

_____

Eᴍᴘʜᴀsɪs—What did the Holy Spirit emphasize to you as you read? (If nothing, you haven't read long enough.)

_____
_____
_____
_____
_____
_____

Rᴇᴘᴇɴᴛ—What do you need to turn away from so that you may DO what you read?

_____
_____
_____
_____
_____

Vᴏʟʟᴇʏ—What are some ways to share what you've learned with others?

_____
_____

Exᴘʀᴇss—Express your praise, your confession, your requests to the Lord.

_____
_____
_____
_____
_____
_____
_____
_____
_____
_____
_____
_____

__Go__ into __All__ the world, __Make__ disciples, __Empowered__ from on high.

The Lineup

(What needs to be accomplished today?)

1. _____
2. _____
3. _____
4. _____
5. _____
6. _____

Subs:

_____

_____

"teach me to number my days"

24 Hours

SCORE SHEET (Recap of the day)

_____
_____
_____
_____
_____
_____
_____
_____
_____
_____
_____
_____
_____
_____

__Go__ into __All__ the world, __Make__ disciples, __Empowered__ from on high.

Date:_____

SCRIPTURE—What Scripture reference(s) are you reading?

_____

EMPHASIS—What did the Holy Spirit emphasize to you as you read? (If nothing, you haven't read long enough.)

_____
_____
_____
_____
_____
_____

REPENT—What do you need to turn away from so that you may DO what you read?

_____
_____
_____
_____
_____

VOLLEY—What are some ways to share what you've learned with others?

_____
_____

EXPRESS—Express your praise, your confession, your requests to the Lord.

_____
_____
_____
_____
_____
_____
_____
_____
_____
_____
_____
_____

__Go__ into __All__ the world, __Make__ disciples, __Empowered__ from on high.

The Lineup

(What needs to be accomplished today?)

1. _____

2. _____

3. _____

4. _____

5. _____

6. _____

Subs:

_____

_____

"teach me to number my days"

24 Hours

SCORE SHEET (Recap of the day)

_____
_____
_____
_____
_____
_____
_____
_____
_____
_____
_____
_____
_____
_____
_____

__Go__ into __All__ the world, __Make__ disciples, __Empowered__ from on high.

Date:_____

SCRIPTURE—What Scripture reference(s) are you reading?

_____

EMPHASIS—What did the Holy Spirit emphasize to you as you read? (If nothing, you haven't read long enough.)

_____
_____
_____
_____
_____
_____

REPENT—What do you need to turn away from so that you may DO what you read?

_____
_____
_____
_____
_____

VOLLEY—What are some ways to share what you've learned with others?

_____
_____

EXPRESS—Express your praise, your confession, your requests to the Lord.

_____
_____
_____
_____
_____
_____
_____
_____
_____
_____
_____
_____

__Go__ into __All__ the world, __Make__ disciples, __Empowered__ from on high.

The Lineup

(What needs to be accomplished today?)

1. _____
2. _____
3. _____
4. _____
5. _____
6. _____

Subs:

_____

_____

"teach me to number my days"

24 Hours

SCORE SHEET (Recap of the day)

_____

_____

_____

_____

_____

_____

_____

_____

_____

_____

_____

_____

_____

_____

__Go__ into __All__ the world, __Make__ disciples, __Empowered__ from on high.

Date:_____

SCRIPTURE—What Scripture reference(s) are you reading?

_____

EMPHASIS—What did the Holy Spirit emphasize to you as you read? (If nothing, you haven't read long enough.)

_____
_____
_____
_____
_____
_____

REPENT—What do you need to turn away from so that you may DO what you read?

_____
_____
_____
_____
_____

VOLLEY—What are some ways to share what you've learned with others?

_____
_____

EXPRESS—Express your praise, your confession, your requests to the Lord.

_____
_____
_____
_____
_____
_____
_____
_____
_____
_____
_____

_**Go**_ into _**All**_ the world, _**Make**_ disciples, _**Empowered**_ from on high.

The Lineup

(What needs to be accomplished today?)

1. _____
2. _____
3. _____
4. _____
5. _____
6. _____

Subs:

_____

_____

"teach me to number my days"

24 Hours

SCORE SHEET (Recap of the day)

_____
_____
_____
_____
_____
_____
_____
_____
_____
_____
_____
_____
_____
_____

__Go__ into __All__ the world, __Make__ disciples, __Empowered__ from on high.

Date:_____

SCRIPTURE—What Scripture reference(s) are you reading?

_____

EMPHASIS—What did the Holy Spirit emphasize to you as you read? (If nothing, you haven't read long enough.)

_____
_____
_____
_____
_____
_____

REPENT—What do you need to turn away from so that you may DO what you read?

_____
_____
_____
_____
_____

VOLLEY—What are some ways to share what you've learned with others?

_____
_____

EXPRESS—Express your praise, your confession, your requests to the Lord.

_____
_____
_____
_____
_____
_____
_____
_____
_____
_____
_____
_____

__Go__ into __All__ the world, __Make__ disciples, __Empowered__ from on high.

The Lineup

(What needs to be accomplished today?)

1. _____

2. _____

3. _____

4. _____

5. _____

6. _____

Subs:

_____

_____

"teach me to number my days"

24 Hours

SCORE SHEET (Recap of the day)

_____
_____
_____
_____
_____
_____
_____
_____
_____
_____
_____
_____
_____
_____
_____
_____
_____

__Go__ into __All__ the world, __Make__ disciples, __Empowered__ from on high.

Date:_____

SCRIPTURE—What Scripture reference(s) are you reading?

_____

EMPHASIS—What did the Holy Spirit emphasize to you as you read? (If nothing, you haven't read long enough.)

_____
_____
_____
_____
_____
_____

REPENT—What do you need to turn away from so that you may DO what you read?

_____
_____
_____
_____
_____

VOLLEY—What are some ways to share what you've learned with others?

_____
_____

EXPRESS—Express your praise, your confession, your requests to the Lord.

_____
_____
_____
_____
_____
_____
_____
_____
_____
_____
_____
_____

_**Go**_ into _**All**_ the world, _**Make**_ disciples, _**Empowered**_ from on high.

The Lineup

(What needs to be accomplished today?)

1. _____

2. _____

3. _____

4. _____

5. _____

6. _____

Subs:

_____

_____

"teach me to number my days"

24 Hours

SCORE SHEET (Recap of the day)

_____
_____
_____
_____
_____
_____
_____
_____
_____
_____
_____
_____
_____
_____

__Go__ into __All__ the world, __Make__ disciples, __Empowered__ from on high.

Date:_____

SCRIPTURE—What Scripture reference(s) are you reading?

_____

EMPHASIS—What did the Holy Spirit emphasize to you as you read? (If nothing, you haven't read long enough.)

_____
_____
_____
_____
_____
_____

REPENT—What do you need to turn away from so that you may DO what you read?

_____
_____
_____
_____
_____

VOLLEY—What are some ways to share what you've learned with others?

_____
_____

EXPRESS—Express your praise, your confession, your requests to the Lord.

_____
_____
_____
_____
_____
_____
_____
_____
_____
_____
_____
_____

**Go** into **All** the world, **Make** disciples, **Empowered** from on high.

The Lineup

(What needs to be accomplished today?)

1. _____

2. _____

3. _____

4. _____

5. _____

6. _____

Subs:

_____

_____

"teach me to number my days"

24 Hours

SCORE SHEET (Recap of the day)

_____
_____
_____
_____
_____
_____
_____
_____
_____
_____
_____
_____
_____
_____
_____

_Go_ into **_All_** the world, **_Make_** disciples, **_Empowered_** from on high.

Date:_____

SCRIPTURE—What Scripture reference(s) are you reading?

_____

EMPHASIS—What did the Holy Spirit emphasize to you as you read? (If nothing, you haven't read long enough.)

_____
_____
_____
_____
_____
_____

REPENT—What do you need to turn away from so that you may DO what you read?

_____
_____
_____
_____
_____

VOLLEY—What are some ways to share what you've learned with others?

_____
_____

EXPRESS—Express your praise, your confession, your requests to the Lord.

_____
_____
_____
_____
_____
_____
_____
_____
_____
_____
_____

__Go__ into __All__ the world, __Make__ disciples, __Empowered__ from on high.

The Lineup

(What needs to be accomplished today?)

1. _____

2. _____

3. _____

4. _____

5. _____

6. _____

Subs:

_____

_____

"teach me to number my days"

24 Hours

SCORE SHEET (Recap of the day)

_____

_____

_____

_____

_____

_____

_____

_____

_____

_____

_____

_____

_____

_____

_____

Go into *All* the world, *Make* disciples, *Empowered* from on high.

Date:_____

SCRIPTURE—What Scripture reference(s) are you reading?

_____

EMPHASIS—What did the Holy Spirit emphasize to you as you read? (If nothing, you haven't read long enough.)

_____
_____
_____
_____
_____
_____

REPENT—What do you need to turn away from so that you may DO what you read?

_____
_____
_____
_____
_____

VOLLEY—What are some ways to share what you've learned with others?

_____
_____

EXPRESS—Express your praise, your confession, your requests to the Lord.

_____
_____
_____
_____
_____
_____
_____
_____
_____
_____
_____
_____

__Go__ into __All__ the world, __Make__ disciples, __Empowered__ from on high.

The Lineup

(What needs to be accomplished today?)

1. _____

2. _____

3. _____

4. _____

5. _____

6. _____

Subs:

_____

_____

"teach me to number my days"

24 Hours

SCORE SHEET (Recap of the day)

_____
_____
_____
_____
_____
_____
_____
_____
_____
_____
_____
_____
_____
_____
_____
_____

__Go__ into __All__ the world, __Make__ disciples, __Empowered__ from on high.

Date:_____

SCRIPTURE—What Scripture reference(s) are you reading?

_____

EMPHASIS—What did the Holy Spirit emphasize to you as you read? (If nothing, you haven't read long enough.)

_____
_____
_____
_____
_____
_____

REPENT—What do you need to turn away from so that you may DO what you read?

_____
_____
_____
_____
_____

VOLLEY—What are some ways to share what you've learned with others?

_____
_____

EXPRESS—Express your praise, your confession, your requests to the Lord.

_____
_____
_____
_____
_____
_____
_____
_____
_____
_____
_____

**Go** into **All** the world, **Make** disciples, **Empowered** from on high.

The Lineup

(What needs to be accomplished today?)

1. _____

2. _____

3. _____

4. _____

5. _____

6. _____

Subs:

_____

_____

"teach me to number my days"

24 Hours

SCORE SHEET (Recap of the day)

_____
_____
_____
_____
_____
_____
_____
_____
_____
_____
_____
_____
_____
_____
_____
_____

__Go__ into __All__ the world, __Make__ disciples, __Empowered__ from on high.

Date:_____

Sᴄʀɪᴘᴛᴜʀᴇ—What Scripture reference(s) are you reading?
_____

Eᴍᴘʜᴀsɪs—What did the Holy Spirit emphasize to you as you read? (If nothing, you haven't read long enough.)
_____
_____
_____
_____
_____
_____

Rᴇᴘᴇɴᴛ—What do you need to turn away from so that you may DO what you read?
_____
_____
_____
_____
_____

Vᴏʟʟᴇʏ—What are some ways to share what you've learned with others?
_____
_____

Exᴘʀᴇss—Express your praise, your confession, your requests to the Lord.
_____
_____
_____
_____
_____
_____
_____
_____
_____
_____
_____
_____
_____
_____

__Go__ into __All__ the world, __Make__ disciples, __Empowered__ from on high.

The Lineup

(What needs to be accomplished today?)

1. _____
2. _____
3. _____
4. _____
5. _____
6. _____

Subs:

_____

_____

"teach me to number my days"

24 Hours

SCORE SHEET (Recap of the day)

_____
_____
_____
_____
_____
_____
_____
_____
_____
_____
_____
_____
_____
_____
_____

__Go__ into __All__ the world, __Make__ disciples, __Empowered__ from on high.

Date:_____

SCRIPTURE—What Scripture reference(s) are you reading?

_____

EMPHASIS—What did the Holy Spirit emphasize to you as you read? (If nothing, you haven't read long enough.)

_____
_____
_____
_____
_____
_____

REPENT—What do you need to turn away from so that you may DO what you read?

_____
_____
_____
_____
_____

VOLLEY—What are some ways to share what you've learned with others?

_____
_____

EXPRESS—Express your praise, your confession, your requests to the Lord.

_____
_____
_____
_____
_____
_____
_____
_____
_____
_____
_____
_____

__Go__ into __All__ the world, __Make__ disciples, __Empowered__ from on high.

The Lineup

(What needs to be accomplished today?)

1. _____

2. _____

3. _____

4. _____

5. _____

6. _____

Subs:

_____

_____

SCORE SHEET (Recap of the day)

_____
_____
_____
_____
_____
_____
_____
_____
_____
_____
_____
_____
_____
_____
_____

**Go** into **All** the world, **Make** disciples, **Empowered** from on high.

Date:_____

SCRIPTURE—What Scripture reference(s) are you reading?

_____

EMPHASIS—What did the Holy Spirit emphasize to you as you read? (If nothing, you haven't read long enough.)

_____
_____
_____
_____
_____
_____

REPENT—What do you need to turn away from so that you may DO what you read?

_____
_____
_____
_____
_____

VOLLEY—What are some ways to share what you've learned with others?

_____
_____

EXPRESS—Express your praise, your confession, your requests to the Lord.

_____
_____
_____
_____
_____
_____
_____
_____
_____
_____
_____
_____

**Go** into **All** the world, **Make** disciples, **Empowered** from on high.

The Lineup

(What needs to be accomplished today?)

1. _____

2. _____

3. _____

4. _____

5. _____

6. _____

Subs:

_____

_____

"teach me to number my days"

24 Hours

SCORE SHEET (Recap of the day)

_____
_____
_____
_____
_____
_____
_____
_____
_____
_____
_____
_____
_____
_____

__Go__ into __All__ the world, __Make__ disciples, __Empowered__ from on high.

Date:_____

SCRIPTURE—What Scripture reference(s) are you reading?

_____

EMPHASIS—What did the Holy Spirit emphasize to you as you read? (If nothing, you haven't read long enough.)

_____
_____
_____
_____
_____
_____

REPENT—What do you need to turn away from so that you may DO what you read?

_____
_____
_____
_____
_____

VOLLEY—What are some ways to share what you've learned with others?

_____
_____

EXPRESS—Express your praise, your confession, your requests to the Lord.

_____
_____
_____
_____
_____
_____
_____
_____
_____
_____
_____
_____

__Go__ into __All__ the world, __Make__ disciples, __Empowered__ from on high.

The Lineup

(What needs to be accomplished today?)

1. _____
2. _____
3. _____
4. _____
5. _____
6. _____

Subs:

_____

_____

"teach me to number my days"

24 Hours

SCORE SHEET (Recap of the day)

_____
_____
_____
_____
_____
_____
_____
_____
_____
_____
_____
_____
_____
_____

__Go__ into *__All__* the world, *__Make__* disciples, *__Empowered__* from on high.

Date:_____

SCRIPTURE—What Scripture reference(s) are you reading?

_____

EMPHASIS—What did the Holy Spirit emphasize to you as you read? (If nothing, you haven't read long enough.)

_____
_____
_____
_____
_____
_____

REPENT—What do you need to turn away from so that you may DO what you read?

_____
_____
_____
_____
_____

VOLLEY—What are some ways to share what you've learned with others?

_____
_____

EXPRESS—Express your praise, your confession, your requests to the Lord.

_____
_____
_____
_____
_____
_____
_____
_____
_____
_____
_____
_____

__Go__ into __All__ the world, __Make__ disciples, __Empowered__ from on high.

The Lineup

(What needs to be accomplished today?)

1. _____
2. _____
3. _____
4. _____
5. _____
6. _____

Subs:

_____

_____

"teach me to number my days"

24 Hours

SCORE SHEET (Recap of the day)

_____
_____
_____
_____
_____
_____
_____
_____
_____
_____
_____
_____
_____
_____
_____

__Go__ into __All__ the world, __Make__ disciples, __Empowered__ from on high.

Date:_____

SCRIPTURE—What Scripture reference(s) are you reading?

_____

EMPHASIS—What did the Holy Spirit emphasize to you as you read? (If nothing, you haven't read long enough.)

_____
_____
_____
_____
_____
_____

REPENT—What do you need to turn away from so that you may DO what you read?

_____
_____
_____
_____
_____

VOLLEY—What are some ways to share what you've learned with others?

_____
_____

EXPRESS—Express your praise, your confession, your requests to the Lord.

_____
_____
_____
_____
_____
_____
_____
_____
_____
_____
_____

**Go** into **All** the world, **Make** disciples, **Empowered** from on high.

The Lineup

(What needs to be accomplished today?)

1. _____
2. _____
3. _____
4. _____
5. _____
6. _____

Subs:

_____

_____

"teach me to number my days"

24 Hours

SCORE SHEET (Recap of the day)

_____
_____
_____
_____
_____
_____
_____
_____
_____
_____
_____
_____
_____
_____
_____
_____

__Go__ into *__All__* the world, *__Make__* disciples, *__Empowered__* from on high.

Date:_____

SCRIPTURE—What Scripture reference(s) are you reading?

_____

EMPHASIS—What did the Holy Spirit emphasize to you as you read? (If nothing, you haven't read long enough.)

_____
_____
_____
_____
_____
_____

REPENT—What do you need to turn away from so that you may DO what you read?

_____
_____
_____
_____
_____

VOLLEY—What are some ways to share what you've learned with others?

_____
_____

EXPRESS—Express your praise, your confession, your requests to the Lord.

_____
_____
_____
_____
_____
_____
_____
_____
_____
_____
_____
_____

__Go__ into __All__ the world, __Make__ disciples, __Empowered__ from on high.

The Lineup

(What needs to be accomplished today?)

1. _____

2. _____

3. _____

4. _____

5. _____

6. _____

Subs:

_____

_____

"teach me to number my days"

24 Hours

SCORE SHEET (Recap of the day)

_____

_____

_____

_____

_____

_____

_____

_____

_____

_____

_____

_____

_____

_____

Go into ***All*** the world, ***Make*** disciples, ***Empowered*** from on high.

Date:_____

SCRIPTURE—What Scripture reference(s) are you reading?

_____

EMPHASIS—What did the Holy Spirit emphasize to you as you read? (If nothing, you haven't read long enough.)

_____
_____
_____
_____
_____
_____

REPENT—What do you need to turn away from so that you may DO what you read?

_____
_____
_____
_____
_____

VOLLEY—What are some ways to share what you've learned with others?

_____
_____

EXPRESS—Express your praise, your confession, your requests to the Lord.

_____
_____
_____
_____
_____
_____
_____
_____
_____
_____
_____
_____

***Go** into **All** the world, **Make** disciples, **Empowered** from on high.*

The Lineup

(What needs to be accomplished today?)

1. _____

2. _____

3. _____

4. _____

5. _____

6. _____

Subs:

_____

_____

"teach me to number my days"

24 Hours

SCORE SHEET (Recap of the day)

_____

_____

_____

_____

_____

_____

_____

_____

_____

_____

_____

_____

_____

_____

**Go** into **All** the world, **Make** disciples, **Empowered** from on high.

Date:_____

SCRIPTURE—What Scripture reference(s) are you reading?

_____

EMPHASIS—What did the Holy Spirit emphasize to you as you read? (If nothing, you haven't read long enough.)

_____
_____
_____
_____
_____
_____

REPENT—What do you need to turn away from so that you may DO what you read?

_____
_____
_____
_____
_____

VOLLEY—What are some ways to share what you've learned with others?

_____
_____

EXPRESS—Express your praise, your confession, your requests to the Lord.

_____
_____
_____
_____
_____
_____
_____
_____
_____
_____
_____
_____

__Go__ into __All__ the world, __Make__ disciples, __Empowered__ from on high.

The Lineup

(What needs to be accomplished today?)

1. _____
2. _____
3. _____
4. _____
5. _____
6. _____

Subs:

_____

_____

"teach me to number my days"

24 Hours

SCORE SHEET (Recap of the day)

_____
_____
_____
_____
_____
_____
_____
_____
_____
_____
_____
_____
_____
_____
_____

Go into *All* the world, *Make* disciples, *Empowered* from on high.

Date:_____

SCRIPTURE—What Scripture reference(s) are you reading?

_____

EMPHASIS—What did the Holy Spirit emphasize to you as you read? (If nothing, you haven't read long enough.)

_____
_____
_____
_____
_____
_____

REPENT—What do you need to turn away from so that you may DO what you read?

_____
_____
_____
_____
_____

VOLLEY—What are some ways to share what you've learned with others?

_____
_____

EXPRESS—Express your praise, your confession, your requests to the Lord.

_____
_____
_____
_____
_____
_____
_____
_____
_____
_____
_____
_____

__Go__ into __All__ the world, __Make__ disciples, __Empowered__ from on high.

The Lineup

(What needs to be accomplished today?)

1. _____

2. _____

3. _____

4. _____

5. _____

6. _____

Subs:

_____

_____

"teach me to number my days"

24 Hours

SCORE SHEET (Recap of the day)

_____
_____
_____
_____
_____
_____
_____
_____
_____
_____
_____
_____
_____
_____
_____
_____

Go into *All* the world, *Make* disciples, *Empowered* from on high.

Date:_____

SCRIPTURE—What Scripture reference(s) are you reading?

_____

EMPHASIS—What did the Holy Spirit emphasize to you as you read? (If nothing, you haven't read long enough.)

_____
_____
_____
_____
_____
_____

REPENT—What do you need to turn away from so that you may DO what you read?

_____
_____
_____
_____
_____

VOLLEY—What are some ways to share what you've learned with others?

_____
_____

EXPRESS—Express your praise, your confession, your requests to the Lord.

_____
_____
_____
_____
_____
_____
_____
_____
_____
_____
_____

__Go__ into __All__ the world, __Make__ disciples, __Empowered__ from on high.

The Lineup

(What needs to be accomplished today?)

1. _____
2. _____
3. _____
4. _____
5. _____
6. _____

Subs:

_____

_____

"teach me to number my days"

24 Hours

SCORE SHEET (Recap of the day)

_____
_____
_____
_____
_____
_____
_____
_____
_____
_____
_____
_____
_____
_____
_____
_____

_**Go**_ into _**All**_ the world, _**Make**_ disciples, _**Empowered**_ from on high.

Date:_____

Scripture—What Scripture reference(s) are you reading?

_____

Emphasis—What did the Holy Spirit emphasize to you as you read? (If nothing, you haven't read long enough.)

_____
_____
_____
_____
_____
_____

Repent—What do you need to turn away from so that you may DO what you read?

_____
_____
_____
_____
_____

Volley—What are some ways to share what you've learned with others?

_____
_____

Express—Express your praise, your confession, your requests to the Lord.

_____
_____
_____
_____
_____
_____
_____
_____
_____
_____
_____

__Go__ into __All__ the world, __Make__ disciples, __Empowered__ from on high.

The Lineup

(What needs to be accomplished today?)

1. _____
2. _____
3. _____
4. _____
5. _____
6. _____

Subs:

_____

_____

"teach me to number my days"

24 Hours

SCORE SHEET (Recap of the day)

_____
_____
_____
_____
_____
_____
_____
_____
_____
_____
_____
_____
_____
_____
_____

__Go__ into __All__ the world, __Make__ disciples, __Empowered__ from on high.

Date:_____

SCRIPTURE—What Scripture reference(s) are you reading?

_____

EMPHASIS—What did the Holy Spirit emphasize to you as you read? (If nothing, you haven't read long enough.)

_____
_____
_____
_____
_____
_____

REPENT—What do you need to turn away from so that you may DO what you read?

_____
_____
_____
_____
_____

VOLLEY—What are some ways to share what you've learned with others?

_____
_____

EXPRESS—Express your praise, your confession, your requests to the Lord.

_____
_____
_____
_____
_____
_____
_____
_____
_____
_____
_____

__Go__ into __All__ the world, __Make__ disciples, __Empowered__ from on high.

The Lineup

(What needs to be accomplished today?)

1. _____
2. _____
3. _____
4. _____
5. _____
6. _____

Subs:

_____

_____

"teach me to number my days"

24 Hours

SCORE SHEET (Recap of the day)

_____
_____
_____
_____
_____
_____
_____
_____
_____
_____
_____
_____
_____
_____

__Go__ into __All__ the world, __Make__ disciples, __Empowered__ from on high.

Date:_____

SCRIPTURE—What Scripture reference(s) are you reading?

_____

EMPHASIS—What did the Holy Spirit emphasize to you as you read? (If nothing, you haven't read long enough.)

_____
_____
_____
_____
_____
_____

REPENT—What do you need to turn away from so that you may DO what you read?

_____
_____
_____
_____
_____

VOLLEY—What are some ways to share what you've learned with others?

_____
_____

EXPRESS—Express your praise, your confession, your requests to the Lord.

_____
_____
_____
_____
_____
_____
_____
_____
_____
_____
_____
_____

__Go__ into __All__ the world, __Make__ disciples, __Empowered__ from on high.

The Lineup

(What needs to be accomplished today?)

1. _____

2. _____

3. _____

4. _____

5. _____

6. _____

Subs:

_____

_____

"teach me to number my days"

24 Hours

SCORE SHEET (Recap of the day)

_____

_____

_____

_____

_____

_____

_____

_____

_____

_____

_____

_____

_____

_____

_**Go**_ into _**All**_ the world, _**Make**_ disciples, _**Empowered**_ from on high.

Date:_____

SCRIPTURE—What Scripture reference(s) are you reading?

_____

EMPHASIS—What did the Holy Spirit emphasize to you as you read? (If nothing, you haven't read long enough.)

_____
_____
_____
_____
_____
_____

REPENT—What do you need to turn away from so that you may DO what you read?

_____
_____
_____
_____
_____

VOLLEY—What are some ways to share what you've learned with others?

_____
_____

EXPRESS—Express your praise, your confession, your requests to the Lord.

_____
_____
_____
_____
_____
_____
_____
_____
_____
_____
_____
_____

__Go__ into __All__ the world, __Make__ disciples, __Empowered__ from on high.

The Lineup

(What needs to be accomplished today?)

1. _____

2. _____

3. _____

4. _____

5. _____

6. _____

Subs:

_____

_____

"teach me to number my days"

24 Hours

SCORE SHEET (Recap of the day)

_____
_____
_____
_____
_____
_____
_____
_____
_____
_____
_____
_____
_____
_____

_Go_ into **_All_** the world, **_Make_** disciples, **_Empowered_** from on high.

Date:_____

S CRIPTURE—What Scripture reference(s) are you reading?

_____

E MPHASIS—What did the Holy Spirit emphasize to you as you read? (If nothing, you haven't read long enough.)

_____
_____
_____
_____
_____
_____

R EPENT—What do you need to turn away from so that you may DO what you read?

_____
_____
_____
_____
_____

V OLLEY—What are some ways to share what you've learned with others?

_____
_____

E XPRESS—Express your praise, your confession, your requests to the Lord.

_____
_____
_____
_____
_____
_____
_____
_____
_____
_____
_____

**Go** into **All** the world, **Make** disciples, **Empowered** from on high.

The Lineup

(What needs to be accomplished today?)

1. _____

2. _____

3. _____

4. _____

5. _____

6. _____

Subs:

_____

_____

"teach me to number my days"

24 Hours

SCORE SHEET (Recap of the day)

_____
_____
_____
_____
_____
_____
_____
_____
_____
_____
_____
_____
_____
_____
_____

__Go__ into __All__ the world, __Make__ disciples, __Empowered__ from on high.

Date:_____

S CRIPTURE—What Scripture reference(s) are you reading?

_____

E MPHASIS—What did the Holy Spirit emphasize to you as you read? (If nothing, you haven't read long enough.)

_____
_____
_____
_____
_____
_____

R EPENT—What do you need to turn away from so that you may DO what you read?

_____
_____
_____
_____
_____

V OLLEY—What are some ways to share what you've learned with others?

_____
_____

E XPRESS—Express your praise, your confession, your requests to the Lord.

_____
_____
_____
_____
_____
_____
_____
_____
_____
_____
_____

__Go__ into __All__ the world, __Make__ disciples, __Empowered__ from on high.

The Lineup

(What needs to be accomplished today?)

1. _____
2. _____
3. _____
4. _____
5. _____
6. _____

Subs:

_____

_____

"teach me to number my days"

24 Hours

SCORE SHEET (Recap of the day)

_____
_____
_____
_____
_____
_____
_____
_____
_____
_____
_____
_____
_____
_____
_____

__Go__ into __All__ the world, __Make__ disciples, __Empowered__ from on high.

Date:_____

SCRIPTURE—What Scripture reference(s) are you reading?

_____

EMPHASIS—What did the Holy Spirit emphasize to you as you read? (If nothing, you haven't read long enough.)

_____
_____
_____
_____
_____
_____

REPENT—What do you need to turn away from so that you may DO what you read?

_____
_____
_____
_____
_____

VOLLEY—What are some ways to share what you've learned with others?

_____
_____

EXPRESS—Express your praise, your confession, your requests to the Lord.

_____
_____
_____
_____
_____
_____
_____
_____
_____
_____
_____
_____

__Go__ into __All__ the world, __Make__ disciples, __Empowered__ from on high.

The Lineup

(What needs to be accomplished today?)

1. _____
2. _____
3. _____
4. _____
5. _____
6. _____

Subs:

_____

_____

"teach me to number my days"

24 Hours

SCORE SHEET (Recap of the day)

_____
_____
_____
_____
_____
_____
_____
_____
_____
_____
_____
_____
_____
_____
_____

__Go__ into __All__ the world, __Make__ disciples, __Empowered__ from on high.

Date:_____

SCRIPTURE—What Scripture reference(s) are you reading?

_____

EMPHASIS—What did the Holy Spirit emphasize to you as you read? (If nothing, you haven't read long enough.)

_____
_____
_____
_____
_____
_____

REPENT—What do you need to turn away from so that you may DO what you read?

_____
_____
_____
_____
_____

VOLLEY—What are some ways to share what you've learned with others?

_____
_____

EXPRESS—Express your praise, your confession, your requests to the Lord.

_____
_____
_____
_____
_____
_____
_____
_____
_____
_____
_____
_____
_____
_____

**Go** into **All** the world, **Make** disciples, **Empowered** from on high.

The Lineup

(What needs to be accomplished today?)

1. _____

2. _____

3. _____

4. _____

5. _____

6. _____

Subs:

_____

_____

"teach me to number my days"

24 Hours

SCORE SHEET (Recap of the day)

_____

_____

_____

_____

_____

_____

_____

_____

_____

_____

_____

_____

_____

_____

_____

_____

__Go__ into __All__ the world, __Make__ disciples, __Empowered__ from on high.

Date:_____

SCRIPTURE—What Scripture reference(s) are you reading?

_____

EMPHASIS—What did the Holy Spirit emphasize to you as you read? (If nothing, you haven't read long enough.)

_____
_____
_____
_____
_____
_____

REPENT—What do you need to turn away from so that you may DO what you read?

_____
_____
_____
_____
_____

VOLLEY—What are some ways to share what you've learned with others?

_____
_____

EXPRESS—Express your praise, your confession, your requests to the Lord.

_____
_____
_____
_____
_____
_____
_____
_____
_____
_____
_____
_____

**Go** into **All** the world, **Make** disciples, **Empowered** from on high.

The Lineup

(What needs to be accomplished today?)

1. _____

2. _____

3. _____

4. _____

5. _____

6. _____

Subs:

_____

_____

SCORE SHEET (Recap of the day)

_____
_____
_____
_____
_____
_____
_____
_____
_____
_____
_____
_____
_____
_____

*<u>**Go**</u> into <u>**All**</u> the world, <u>***Make***</u> disciples, <u>***Empowered***</u> from on high.*

Date:_____

SCRIPTURE—What Scripture reference(s) are you reading?

_____

EMPHASIS—What did the Holy Spirit emphasize to you as you read? (If nothing, you haven't read long enough.)

_____
_____
_____
_____
_____
_____

REPENT—What do you need to turn away from so that you may DO what you read?

_____
_____
_____
_____
_____

VOLLEY—What are some ways to share what you've learned with others?

_____
_____

EXPRESS—Express your praise, your confession, your requests to the Lord.

_____
_____
_____
_____
_____
_____
_____
_____
_____
_____
_____

__Go__ into __All__ the world, __Make__ disciples, __Empowered__ from on high.

The Lineup

(What needs to be accomplished today?)

1. _____
2. _____
3. _____
4. _____
5. _____
6. _____

Subs:

_____

_____

SCORE SHEET (Recap of the day)

_____

_____

_____

_____

_____

_____

_____

_____

_____

_____

_____

_____

_____

_____

_____

__Go__ into *__All__* the world, *__Make__* disciples, *__Empowered__* from on high.

Date:_____

SCRIPTURE—What Scripture reference(s) are you reading?

_____

EMPHASIS—What did the Holy Spirit emphasize to you as you read? (If nothing, you haven't read long enough.)

_____
_____
_____
_____
_____
_____

REPENT—What do you need to turn away from so that you may DO what you read?

_____
_____
_____
_____
_____

VOLLEY—What are some ways to share what you've learned with others?

_____
_____

EXPRESS—Express your praise, your confession, your requests to the Lord.

_____
_____
_____
_____
_____
_____
_____
_____
_____
_____
_____
_____

__Go__ into __All__ the world, __Make__ disciples, __Empowered__ from on high.

The Lineup

(What needs to be accomplished today?)

1. _____
2. _____
3. _____
4. _____
5. _____
6. _____

Subs:

_____

_____

"teach me to number my days"

24 Hours

SCORE SHEET (Recap of the day)

_____
_____
_____
_____
_____
_____
_____
_____
_____
_____
_____
_____
_____
_____
_____

__Go__ into __All__ the world, __Make__ disciples, __Empowered__ from on high.

Date:_____

SCRIPTURE—What Scripture reference(s) are you reading?

_____

EMPHASIS—What did the Holy Spirit emphasize to you as you read? (If nothing, you haven't read long enough.)

_____
_____
_____
_____
_____
_____

REPENT—What do you need to turn away from so that you may DO what you read?

_____
_____
_____
_____
_____

VOLLEY—What are some ways to share what you've learned with others?

_____
_____

EXPRESS—Express your praise, your confession, your requests to the Lord.

_____
_____
_____
_____
_____
_____
_____
_____
_____
_____
_____

_**Go**_ into _**All**_ the world, _**Make**_ disciples, _**Empowered**_ from on high.

The Lineup

(What needs to be accomplished today?)

1. _____
2. _____
3. _____
4. _____
5. _____
6. _____

Subs:

_____

_____

SCORE SHEET (Recap of the day)

_____
_____
_____
_____
_____
_____
_____
_____
_____
_____
_____
_____
_____
_____
_____
_____

__Go__ into __All__ the world, __Make__ disciples, __Empowered__ from on high.

Date:_____

SCRIPTURE—What Scripture reference(s) are you reading?

_____

EMPHASIS—What did the Holy Spirit emphasize to you as you read? (If nothing, you haven't read long enough.)

_____
_____
_____
_____
_____
_____

REPENT—What do you need to turn away from so that you may DO what you read?

_____
_____
_____
_____
_____

VOLLEY—What are some ways to share what you've learned with others?

_____
_____

EXPRESS—Express your praise, your confession, your requests to the Lord.

_____
_____
_____
_____
_____
_____
_____
_____
_____
_____
_____

__Go__ into __All__ the world, __Make__ disciples, __Empowered__ from on high.

The Lineup

(What needs to be accomplished today?)

1. _____
2. _____
3. _____
4. _____
5. _____
6. _____

Subs:

_____

_____

"teach me to number my days"

24 Hours

SCORE SHEET (Recap of the day)

_____
_____
_____
_____
_____
_____
_____
_____
_____
_____
_____
_____
_____
_____
_____
_____

__Go__ into __All__ the world, __Make__ disciples, __Empowered__ from on high.

Date:_____

SCRIPTURE—What Scripture reference(s) are you reading?

_____

EMPHASIS—What did the Holy Spirit emphasize to you as you read? (If nothing, you haven't read long enough.)

_____
_____
_____
_____
_____
_____

REPENT—What do you need to turn away from so that you may DO what you read?

_____
_____
_____
_____

VOLLEY—What are some ways to share what you've learned with others?

_____
_____

EXPRESS—Express your praise, your confession, your requests to the Lord.

_____
_____
_____
_____
_____
_____
_____
_____
_____
_____
_____

__Go__ into __All__ the world, __Make__ disciples, __Empowered__ from on high.

The Lineup

(What needs to be accomplished today?)

1. _____

2. _____

3. _____

4. _____

5. _____

6. _____

Subs:

_____

_____

"teach me to number my days"
24 Hours

SCORE SHEET (Recap of the day)

_____
_____
_____
_____
_____
_____
_____
_____
_____
_____
_____
_____
_____
_____
_____
_____

__Go__ into __All__ the world, __Make__ disciples, __Empowered__ from on high.

Date:_____

SCRIPTURE—What Scripture reference(s) are you reading?

_____

EMPHASIS—What did the Holy Spirit emphasize to you as you read? (If nothing, you haven't read long enough.)

_____
_____
_____
_____
_____
_____

REPENT—What do you need to turn away from so that you may DO what you read?

_____
_____
_____
_____
_____

VOLLEY—What are some ways to share what you've learned with others?

_____
_____

EXPRESS—Express your praise, your confession, your requests to the Lord.

_____
_____
_____
_____
_____
_____
_____
_____
_____
_____
_____

__Go__ into __All__ the world, __Make__ disciples, __Empowered__ from on high.

The Lineup

(What needs to be accomplished today?)

1. _____

2. _____

3. _____

4. _____

5. _____

6. _____

Subs:

_____

_____

"teach me to number my days"

24 Hours

SCORE SHEET (Recap of the day)

_____

_____

_____

_____

_____

_____

_____

_____

_____

_____

_____

_____

_____

_____

_____

_____

_**Go**_ into _**All**_ the world, _**Make**_ disciples, _**Empowered**_ from on high.

Date:_____

SCRIPTURE—What Scripture reference(s) are you reading?

_____

EMPHASIS—What did the Holy Spirit emphasize to you as you read? (If nothing, you haven't read long enough.)

_____
_____
_____
_____
_____
_____

REPENT—What do you need to turn away from so that you may DO what you read?

_____
_____
_____
_____
_____

VOLLEY—What are some ways to share what you've learned with others?

_____
_____

EXPRESS—Express your praise, your confession, your requests to the Lord.

_____
_____
_____
_____
_____
_____
_____
_____
_____
_____
_____
_____

__Go__ into __All__ the world, __Make__ disciples, __Empowered__ from on high.

The Lineup

(What needs to be accomplished today?)

1. _____

2. _____

3. _____

4. _____

5. _____

6. _____

Subs:

_____

_____

"teach me to number my days"

24 Hours

SCORE SHEET (Recap of the day)

_____
_____
_____
_____
_____
_____
_____
_____
_____
_____
_____
_____
_____
_____

***Go** into **All** the world, **Make** disciples, **Empowered** from on high.*

Date:_____

SCRIPTURE—What Scripture reference(s) are you reading?

_____

EMPHASIS—What did the Holy Spirit emphasize to you as you read? (If nothing, you haven't read long enough.)

_____
_____
_____
_____
_____
_____

REPENT—What do you need to turn away from so that you may DO what you read?

_____
_____
_____
_____
_____

VOLLEY—What are some ways to share what you've learned with others?

_____
_____

EXPRESS—Express your praise, your confession, your requests to the Lord.

_____
_____
_____
_____
_____
_____
_____
_____
_____
_____
_____
_____

_**Go**_ into _**All**_ the world, _**Make**_ disciples, _**Empowered**_ from on high.

The Lineup

(What needs to be accomplished today?)

1. _____

2. _____

3. _____

4. _____

5. _____

6. _____

Subs:

_____

_____

"teach me to number my days"

24 Hours

SCORE SHEET (Recap of the day)

_____
_____
_____
_____
_____
_____
_____
_____
_____
_____
_____
_____
_____
_____
_____

Go into ***All*** the world, ***Make*** disciples, ***Empowered*** from on high.

Date:_____

SCRIPTURE—What Scripture reference(s) are you reading?

_____

EMPHASIS—What did the Holy Spirit emphasize to you as you read? (If nothing, you haven't read long enough.)

_____
_____
_____
_____
_____
_____

REPENT—What do you need to turn away from so that you may DO what you read?

_____
_____
_____
_____
_____

VOLLEY—What are some ways to share what you've learned with others?

_____
_____

EXPRESS—Express your praise, your confession, your requests to the Lord.

_____
_____
_____
_____
_____
_____
_____
_____
_____
_____
_____

__Go__ into __All__ the world, __Make__ disciples, __Empowered__ from on high.

The Lineup

(What needs to be accomplished today?)

1. _____

2. _____

3. _____

4. _____

5. _____

6. _____

Subs:

_____

_____

"teach me to number my days"

24 Hours

SCORE SHEET (Recap of the day)

_____
_____
_____
_____
_____
_____
_____
_____
_____
_____
_____
_____
_____

__Go__ into __All__ the world, __Make__ disciples, __Empowered__ from on high.

Date:_____

SCRIPTURE—What Scripture reference(s) are you reading?

_____

EMPHASIS—What did the Holy Spirit emphasize to you as you read? (If nothing, you haven't read long enough.)

_____
_____
_____
_____
_____
_____

REPENT—What do you need to turn away from so that you may DO what you read?

_____
_____
_____
_____
_____

VOLLEY—What are some ways to share what you've learned with others?

_____
_____

EXPRESS—Express your praise, your confession, your requests to the Lord.

_____
_____
_____
_____
_____
_____
_____
_____
_____
_____
_____

**Go** into **All** the world, **Make** disciples, **Empowered** from on high.

The Lineup

(What needs to be accomplished today?)

1. _____

2. _____

3. _____

4. _____

5. _____

6. _____

Subs:

_____

_____

"teach me to number my days"

24 Hours

SCORE SHEET (Recap of the day)

_____
_____
_____
_____
_____
_____
_____
_____
_____
_____
_____
_____
_____
_____
_____

__Go__ into __All__ the world, __Make__ disciples, __Empowered__ from on high.

Date:_____

SCRIPTURE—What Scripture reference(s) are you reading?

_____

EMPHASIS—What did the Holy Spirit emphasize to you as you read? (If nothing, you haven't read long enough.)

_____
_____
_____
_____
_____
_____

REPENT—What do you need to turn away from so that you may DO what you read?

_____
_____
_____
_____
_____

VOLLEY—What are some ways to share what you've learned with others?

_____
_____

EXPRESS—Express your praise, your confession, your requests to the Lord.

_____
_____
_____
_____
_____
_____
_____
_____
_____
_____
_____

__Go__ into __All__ the world, __Make__ disciples, __Empowered__ from on high.

The Lineup

(What needs to be accomplished today?)

1. _____

2. _____

3. _____

4. _____

5. _____

6. _____

Subs:

_____

_____

"teach me to number my days"

24 Hours

SCORE SHEET (Recap of the day)

_____
_____
_____
_____
_____
_____
_____
_____
_____
_____
_____
_____
_____
_____
_____
_____

***Go** into **All** the world, **Make** disciples, **Empowered** from on high.*

Date:_____

SCRIPTURE—What Scripture reference(s) are you reading?

_____

EMPHASIS—What did the Holy Spirit emphasize to you as you read? (If nothing, you haven't read long enough.)

_____
_____
_____
_____
_____
_____

REPENT—What do you need to turn away from so that you may DO what you read?

_____
_____
_____
_____
_____

VOLLEY—What are some ways to share what you've learned with others?

_____
_____

EXPRESS—Express your praise, your confession, your requests to the Lord.

_____
_____
_____
_____
_____
_____
_____
_____
_____
_____
_____

**Go** into **All** the world, **Make** disciples, **Empowered** from on high.

The Lineup

(What needs to be accomplished today?)

1. _____
2. _____
3. _____
4. _____
5. _____
6. _____

Subs:

_____

_____

SCORE SHEET (Recap of the day)

_____
_____
_____
_____
_____
_____
_____
_____
_____
_____
_____
_____
_____
_____
_____
_____

__Go__ into __All__ the world, __Make__ disciples, __Empowered__ from on high.

Date:_____

SCRIPTURE—What Scripture reference(s) are you reading?

_____

EMPHASIS—What did the Holy Spirit emphasize to you as you read? (If nothing, you haven't read long enough.)

_____
_____
_____
_____
_____
_____

REPENT—What do you need to turn away from so that you may DO what you read?

_____
_____
_____
_____
_____

VOLLEY—What are some ways to share what you've learned with others?

_____
_____

EXPRESS—Express your praise, your confession, your requests to the Lord.

_____
_____
_____
_____
_____
_____
_____
_____
_____
_____
_____
_____

_**Go**_ into _**All**_ the world, _**Make**_ disciples, _**Empowered**_ from on high.

The Lineup

(What needs to be accomplished today?)

1. _____

2. _____

3. _____

4. _____

5. _____

6. _____

Subs:

_____

_____

"teach me to number my days"

24 Hours

SCORE SHEET (Recap of the day)

_____
_____
_____
_____
_____
_____
_____
_____
_____
_____
_____
_____
_____
_____

_Go_ into _All_ the world, _Make_ disciples, _Empowered_ from on high.

Date:_____

SCRIPTURE—What Scripture reference(s) are you reading?

_____

EMPHASIS—What did the Holy Spirit emphasize to you as you read? (If nothing, you haven't read long enough.)

_____
_____
_____
_____
_____
_____

REPENT—What do you need to turn away from so that you may DO what you read?

_____
_____
_____
_____
_____

VOLLEY—What are some ways to share what you've learned with others?

_____
_____

EXPRESS—Express your praise, your confession, your requests to the Lord.

_____
_____
_____
_____
_____
_____
_____
_____
_____
_____
_____
_____
_____

***Go** into **All** the world, **Make** disciples, **Empowered** from on high.*

The Lineup

(What needs to be accomplished today?)

1. _____
2. _____
3. _____
4. _____
5. _____
6. _____

Subs:

_____

_____

"teach me to number my days"

24 Hours

SCORE SHEET (Recap of the day)

_____
_____
_____
_____
_____
_____
_____
_____
_____
_____
_____
_____
_____
_____
_____

__Go__ into __All__ the world, __Make__ disciples, __Empowered__ from on high.

Date:_____

SCRIPTURE—What Scripture reference(s) are you reading?

_____

EMPHASIS—What did the Holy Spirit emphasize to you as you read? (If nothing, you haven't read long enough.)

_____
_____
_____
_____
_____
_____

REPENT—What do you need to turn away from so that you may DO what you read?

_____
_____
_____
_____
_____

VOLLEY—What are some ways to share what you've learned with others?

_____
_____

EXPRESS—Express your praise, your confession, your requests to the Lord.

_____
_____
_____
_____
_____
_____
_____
_____
_____
_____
_____
_____

__Go__ into __All__ the world, __Make__ disciples, __Empowered__ from on high.

The Lineup

(What needs to be accomplished today?)

1. _____
2. _____
3. _____
4. _____
5. _____
6. _____

Subs:

_____

_____

"teach me to number my days"

24 Hours

SCORE SHEET (Recap of the day)

_____

_____

_____

_____

_____

_____

_____

_____

_____

_____

_____

_____

_____

_____

_____

***Go** into **All** the world, **Make** disciples, **Empowered** from on high.*

Date:_____

SCRIPTURE—What Scripture reference(s) are you reading?

_____

EMPHASIS—What did the Holy Spirit emphasize to you as you read? (If nothing, you haven't read long enough.)

_____
_____
_____
_____
_____
_____

REPENT—What do you need to turn away from so that you may DO what you read?

_____
_____
_____
_____
_____

VOLLEY—What are some ways to share what you've learned with others?

_____
_____

EXPRESS—Express your praise, your confession, your requests to the Lord.

_____
_____
_____
_____
_____
_____
_____
_____
_____
_____
_____
_____

__Go__ into __All__ the world, __Make__ disciples, __Empowered__ from on high.

The Lineup

(What needs to be accomplished today?)

1. _____
2. _____
3. _____
4. _____
5. _____
6. _____

Subs:

_____

_____

"teach me to number my days"

24 Hours

SCORE SHEET (Recap of the day)

_____
_____
_____
_____
_____
_____
_____
_____
_____
_____
_____
_____
_____
_____
_____

__Go__ into __All__ the world, __Make__ disciples, __Empowered__ from on high.

Date:_____

SCRIPTURE—What Scripture reference(s) are you reading?

_____

EMPHASIS—What did the Holy Spirit emphasize to you as you read? (If nothing, you haven't read long enough.)

_____
_____
_____
_____
_____
_____

REPENT—What do you need to turn away from so that you may DO what you read?

_____
_____
_____
_____
_____

VOLLEY—What are some ways to share what you've learned with others?

_____
_____

EXPRESS—Express your praise, your confession, your requests to the Lord.

_____
_____
_____
_____
_____
_____
_____
_____
_____
_____
_____
_____
_____

__Go__ into __All__ the world, __Make__ disciples, __Empowered__ from on high.

The Lineup

(What needs to be accomplished today?)

1. _____

2. _____

3. _____

4. _____

5. _____

6. _____

Subs:

_____

_____

"teach me to number my days"

24 Hours

SCORE SHEET (Recap of the day)

_____

_____

_____

_____

_____

_____

_____

_____

_____

_____

_____

_____

_____

_____

_____

***Go** into **All** the world, **Make** disciples, **Empowered** from on high.*

Date:_____

SCRIPTURE—What Scripture reference(s) are you reading?

_____

EMPHASIS—What did the Holy Spirit emphasize to you as you read? (If nothing, you haven't read long enough.)

_____
_____
_____
_____
_____
_____

REPENT—What do you need to turn away from so that you may DO what you read?

_____
_____
_____
_____
_____

VOLLEY—What are some ways to share what you've learned with others?

_____
_____

EXPRESS—Express your praise, your confession, your requests to the Lord.

_____
_____
_____
_____
_____
_____
_____
_____
_____
_____
_____

__Go__ into __All__ the world, __Make__ disciples, __Empowered__ from on high.

The Lineup

(What needs to be accomplished today?)

1. _____
2. _____
3. _____
4. _____
5. _____
6. _____

Subs:

_____

_____

"teach me to number my days"

24 Hours

SCORE SHEET (Recap of the day)

_____
_____
_____
_____
_____
_____
_____
_____
_____
_____
_____
_____
_____
_____
_____

__Go__ into __All__ the world, __Make__ disciples, __Empowered__ from on high.

Date:_____

SCRIPTURE—What Scripture reference(s) are you reading?

_____

EMPHASIS—What did the Holy Spirit emphasize to you as you read? (If nothing, you haven't read long enough.)

_____
_____
_____
_____
_____
_____

REPENT—What do you need to turn away from so that you may DO what you read?

_____
_____
_____
_____
_____

VOLLEY—What are some ways to share what you've learned with others?

_____
_____

EXPRESS—Express your praise, your confession, your requests to the Lord.

_____
_____
_____
_____
_____
_____
_____
_____
_____
_____
_____
_____

***Go** into **All** the world, **Make** disciples, **Empowered** from on high.*

The Lineup

(What needs to be accomplished today?)

1. _____

2. _____

3. _____

4. _____

5. _____

6. _____

Subs:

_____

_____

SCORE SHEET (Recap of the day)

_____
_____
_____
_____
_____
_____
_____
_____
_____
_____
_____
_____
_____
_____

__Go__ into __All__ the world, __Make__ disciples, __Empowered__ from on high.

Date:_____

SCRIPTURE—What Scripture reference(s) are you reading?

_____

EMPHASIS—What did the Holy Spirit emphasize to you as you read? (If nothing, you haven't read long enough.)

_____
_____
_____
_____
_____
_____

REPENT—What do you need to turn away from so that you may DO what you read?

_____
_____
_____
_____
_____

VOLLEY—What are some ways to share what you've learned with others?

_____
_____

EXPRESS—Express your praise, your confession, your requests to the Lord.

_____
_____
_____
_____
_____
_____
_____
_____
_____
_____
_____

__Go__ into __All__ the world, __Make__ disciples, __Empowered__ from on high.

The Lineup

(What needs to be accomplished today?)

1. _____
2. _____
3. _____
4. _____
5. _____
6. _____

Subs:

_____

_____

"teach me to number my days"

24 Hours

SCORE SHEET (Recap of the day)

_____
_____
_____
_____
_____
_____
_____
_____
_____
_____
_____
_____
_____
_____
_____
_____

Go into *All* the world, *Make* disciples, *Empowered* from on high.

Date:_____

SCRIPTURE—What Scripture reference(s) are you reading?

_____

EMPHASIS—What did the Holy Spirit emphasize to you as you read? (If nothing, you haven't read long enough.)

_____
_____
_____
_____
_____
_____

REPENT—What do you need to turn away from so that you may DO what you read?

_____
_____
_____
_____
_____

VOLLEY—What are some ways to share what you've learned with others?

_____
_____

EXPRESS—Express your praise, your confession, your requests to the Lord.

_____
_____
_____
_____
_____
_____
_____
_____
_____
_____
_____
_____

_**Go**_ into _**All**_ the world, _**Make**_ disciples, _**Empowered**_ from on high.

The Lineup

(What needs to be accomplished today?)

1. _____
2. _____
3. _____
4. _____
5. _____
6. _____

Subs:

_____

_____

SCORE SHEET (Recap of the day)

_____
_____
_____
_____
_____
_____
_____
_____
_____
_____
_____
_____
_____
_____
_____

**Go** into **All** the world, **Make** disciples, **Empowered** from on high.

Date:_____

S CRIPTURE—What Scripture reference(s) are you reading?

_____

E MPHASIS—What did the Holy Spirit emphasize to you as you read? (If nothing, you haven't read long enough.)

_____
_____
_____
_____
_____
_____

R EPENT—What do you need to turn away from so that you may DO what you read?

_____
_____
_____
_____
_____

V OLLEY—What are some ways to share what you've learned with others?

_____
_____

E XPRESS—Express your praise, your confession, your requests to the Lord.

_____
_____
_____
_____
_____
_____
_____
_____
_____
_____
_____
_____
_____

**Go** into **All** the world, **Make** disciples, **Empowered** from on high.

The Lineup

(What needs to be accomplished today?)

1. _____
2. _____
3. _____
4. _____
5. _____
6. _____

Subs:

_____

_____

"teach me to number my days"

24 Hours

SCORE SHEET (Recap of the day)

_____
_____
_____
_____
_____
_____
_____
_____
_____
_____
_____
_____
_____
_____

__Go__ into __All__ the world, __Make__ disciples, __Empowered__ from on high.

Date:_____

S CRIPTURE—What Scripture reference(s) are you reading?

_____

E MPHASIS—What did the Holy Spirit emphasize to you as you read? (If nothing, you haven't read long enough.)

_____
_____
_____
_____
_____
_____

R EPENT—What do you need to turn away from so that you may DO what you read?

_____
_____
_____
_____
_____

V OLLEY—What are some ways to share what you've learned with others?

_____
_____

E XPRESS—Express your praise, your confession, your requests to the Lord.

_____
_____
_____
_____
_____
_____
_____
_____
_____
_____
_____

__Go__ into __All__ the world, __Make__ disciples, __Empowered__ from on high.

The Lineup

(What needs to be accomplished today?)

1. _____

2. _____

3. _____

4. _____

5. _____

6. _____

Subs:

_____

_____

"teach me to number my days"

24 Hours

SCORE SHEET (Recap of the day)

_____

_____

_____

_____

_____

_____

_____

_____

_____

_____

_____

_____

_____

_**Go**_ into _**All**_ the world, _**Make**_ disciples, _**Empowered**_ from on high.

Date:_____

Sᴄʀɪᴘᴛᴜʀᴇ—What Scripture reference(s) are you reading?

_____

Eᴍᴘʜᴀsɪs—What did the Holy Spirit emphasize to you as you read? (If nothing, you haven't read long enough.)

_____
_____
_____
_____
_____
_____

Rᴇᴘᴇɴᴛ—What do you need to turn away from so that you may DO what you read?

_____
_____
_____
_____
_____

Vᴏʟʟᴇʏ—What are some ways to share what you've learned with others?

_____
_____

Exᴘʀᴇss—Express your praise, your confession, your requests to the Lord.

_____
_____
_____
_____
_____
_____
_____
_____
_____
_____
_____

Go into *All* the world, *Make* disciples, *Empowered* from on high.

The Lineup

(What needs to be accomplished today?)

1. _____

2. _____

3. _____

4. _____

5. _____

6. _____

Subs:

_____

_____

SCORE SHEET (Recap of the day)

_____

_____

_____

_____

_____

_____

_____

_____

_____

_____

_____

_____

_____

_____

__Go__ into __All__ the world, __Make__ disciples, __Empowered__ from on high.

Date:_____

SCRIPTURE—What Scripture reference(s) are you reading?

_____

EMPHASIS—What did the Holy Spirit emphasize to you as you read? (If nothing, you haven't read long enough.)

_____
_____
_____
_____
_____
_____

REPENT—What do you need to turn away from so that you may DO what you read?

_____
_____
_____
_____
_____

VOLLEY—What are some ways to share what you've learned with others?

_____
_____

EXPRESS—Express your praise, your confession, your requests to the Lord.

_____
_____
_____
_____
_____
_____
_____
_____
_____
_____
_____
_____

__Go__ into __All__ the world, __Make__ disciples, __Empowered__ from on high.

The Lineup

(What needs to be accomplished today?)

1. _____
2. _____
3. _____
4. _____
5. _____
6. _____

Subs:

_____

_____

"teach me to number my days"

24 Hours

SCORE SHEET (Recap of the day)

_____
_____
_____
_____
_____
_____
_____
_____
_____
_____
_____
_____
_____
_____

__Go__ into __All__ the world, __Make__ disciples, __Empowered__ from on high.

Date:_____

SCRIPTURE—What Scripture reference(s) are you reading?

_____

EMPHASIS—What did the Holy Spirit emphasize to you as you read? (If nothing, you haven't read long enough.)

_____
_____
_____
_____
_____
_____

REPENT—What do you need to turn away from so that you may DO what you read?

_____
_____
_____
_____
_____

VOLLEY—What are some ways to share what you've learned with others?

_____
_____

EXPRESS—Express your praise, your confession, your requests to the Lord.

_____
_____
_____
_____
_____
_____
_____
_____
_____
_____
_____

__Go__ into __All__ the world, __Make__ disciples, __Empowered__ from on high.

The Lineup

(What needs to be accomplished today?)

1. _____
2. _____
3. _____
4. _____
5. _____
6. _____

Subs:

_____

_____

"teach me to number my days"

24 Hours

SCORE SHEET (Recap of the day)

_____
_____
_____
_____
_____
_____
_____
_____
_____
_____
_____
_____
_____
_____
_____
_____

_Go_ into **_All_** the world, **_Make_** disciples, **_Empowered_** from on high.

Date:_____

SCRIPTURE—What Scripture reference(s) are you reading?

_____

EMPHASIS—What did the Holy Spirit emphasize to you as you read? (If nothing, you haven't read long enough.)

_____
_____
_____
_____
_____
_____

REPENT—What do you need to turn away from so that you may DO what you read?

_____
_____
_____
_____
_____

VOLLEY—What are some ways to share what you've learned with others?

_____
_____

EXPRESS—Express your praise, your confession, your requests to the Lord.

_____
_____
_____
_____
_____
_____
_____
_____
_____
_____
_____

Go into *All* the world, *Make* disciples, *Empowered* from on high.

The Lineup

(What needs to be accomplished today?)

1. _____
2. _____
3. _____
4. _____
5. _____
6. _____

Subs:

_____

_____

"teach me to number my days"

24 Hours

SCORE SHEET (Recap of the day)

_____
_____
_____
_____
_____
_____
_____
_____
_____
_____
_____
_____
_____
_____
_____

__Go__ into __All__ the world, __Make__ disciples, __Empowered__ from on high.

Date:_____

Sᴄʀɪᴘᴛᴜʀᴇ—What Scripture reference(s) are you reading?

_____

Eᴍᴘʜᴀꜱɪꜱ—What did the Holy Spirit emphasize to you as you read? (If nothing, you haven't read long enough.)

_____
_____
_____
_____
_____
_____

Rᴇᴘᴇɴᴛ—What do you need to turn away from so that you may DO what you read?

_____
_____
_____
_____
_____

Vᴏʟʟᴇʏ—What are some ways to share what you've learned with others?

_____
_____

Exᴘʀᴇꜱꜱ—Express your praise, your confession, your requests to the Lord.

_____
_____
_____
_____
_____
_____
_____
_____
_____
_____
_____

**Go** into **All** the world, **Make** disciples, **Empowered** from on high.

The Lineup

(What needs to be accomplished today?)

1. _____
2. _____
3. _____
4. _____
5. _____
6. _____

Subs:

_____

_____

SCORE SHEET (Recap of the day)

_____
_____
_____
_____
_____
_____
_____
_____
_____
_____
_____
_____
_____
_____
_____

__Go__ into __All__ the world, __Make__ disciples, __Empowered__ from on high.

Date:_____

SCRIPTURE—What Scripture reference(s) are you reading?

_____

EMPHASIS—What did the Holy Spirit emphasize to you as you read? (If nothing, you haven't read long enough.)

_____
_____
_____
_____
_____
_____

REPENT—What do you need to turn away from so that you may DO what you read?

_____
_____
_____
_____
_____

VOLLEY—What are some ways to share what you've learned with others?

_____
_____

EXPRESS—Express your praise, your confession, your requests to the Lord.

_____
_____
_____
_____
_____
_____
_____
_____
_____
_____
_____
_____

__Go__ into __All__ the world, __Make__ disciples, __Empowered__ from on high.

The Lineup

(What needs to be accomplished today?)

1. _____
2. _____
3. _____
4. _____
5. _____
6. _____

Subs:

_____

_____

"teach me to number my days"

24 Hours

SCORE SHEET (Recap of the day)

_____
_____
_____
_____
_____
_____
_____
_____
_____
_____
_____
_____
_____
_____

__Go__ into __All__ the world, __Make__ disciples, __Empowered__ from on high.

Date:_____

S CRIPTURE—What Scripture reference(s) are you reading?

_____

E MPHASIS—What did the Holy Spirit emphasize to you as you read? (If nothing, you haven't read long enough.)

_____
_____
_____
_____
_____
_____

R EPENT—What do you need to turn away from so that you may DO what you read?

_____
_____
_____
_____

V OLLEY—What are some ways to share what you've learned with others?

_____
_____

E XPRESS—Express your praise, your confession, your requests to the Lord.

_____
_____
_____
_____
_____
_____
_____
_____
_____
_____
_____
_____
_____

__Go__ into __All__ the world, __Make__ disciples, __Empowered__ from on high.

The Lineup

(What needs to be accomplished today?)

1. _____

2. _____

3. _____

4. _____

5. _____

6. _____

Subs:

_____

_____

"teach me to number my days"

24 Hours

SCORE SHEET (Recap of the day)

_____

_____

_____

_____

_____

_____

_____

_____

_____

_____

_____

_____

_____

_____

__Go__ into __All__ the world, __Make__ disciples, __Empowered__ from on high.

Date:_____

SCRIPTURE—What Scripture reference(s) are you reading?

_____

EMPHASIS—What did the Holy Spirit emphasize to you as you read? (If nothing, you haven't read long enough.)

_____
_____
_____
_____
_____
_____

REPENT—What do you need to turn away from so that you may DO what you read?

_____
_____
_____
_____

VOLLEY—What are some ways to share what you've learned with others?

_____
_____

EXPRESS—Express your praise, your confession, your requests to the Lord.

_____
_____
_____
_____
_____
_____
_____
_____
_____
_____
_____

__Go__ into __All__ the world, __Make__ disciples, __Empowered__ from on high.

The Lineup

(What needs to be accomplished today?)

1. _____
2. _____
3. _____
4. _____
5. _____
6. _____

Subs:

_____

_____

"teach me to number my days"

24 Hours

SCORE SHEET (Recap of the day)

_____
_____
_____
_____
_____
_____
_____
_____
_____
_____
_____
_____
_____
_____

__Go__ into __All__ the world, __Make__ disciples, __Empowered__ from on high.

Date:_____

SCRIPTURE—What Scripture reference(s) are you reading?

_____

EMPHASIS—What did the Holy Spirit emphasize to you as you read? (If nothing, you haven't read long enough.)

_____
_____
_____
_____
_____
_____

REPENT—What do you need to turn away from so that you may DO what you read?

_____
_____
_____
_____
_____

VOLLEY—What are some ways to share what you've learned with others?

_____
_____

EXPRESS—Express your praise, your confession, your requests to the Lord.

_____
_____
_____
_____
_____
_____
_____
_____
_____
_____
_____
_____

__Go__ into __All__ the world, __Make__ disciples, __Empowered__ from on high.

The Lineup

(What needs to be accomplished today?)

1. _____
2. _____
3. _____
4. _____
5. _____
6. _____

Subs:

_____

_____

"teach me to number my days"

24 Hours

SCORE SHEET (Recap of the day)

_____

_____

_____

_____

_____

_____

_____

_____

_____

_____

_____

_____

_____

_____

**Go** into **All** the world, **Make** disciples, **Empowered** from on high.

Date:_____

SCRIPTURE—What Scripture reference(s) are you reading?

_____

EMPHASIS—What did the Holy Spirit emphasize to you as you read? (If nothing, you haven't read long enough.)

_____
_____
_____
_____
_____
_____

REPENT—What do you need to turn away from so that you may DO what you read?

_____
_____
_____
_____
_____

VOLLEY—What are some ways to share what you've learned with others?

_____
_____

EXPRESS—Express your praise, your confession, your requests to the Lord.

_____
_____
_____
_____
_____
_____
_____
_____
_____
_____
_____
_____

__Go__ into __All__ the world, __Make__ disciples, __Empowered__ from on high.

The Lineup

(What needs to be accomplished today?)

1. _____
2. _____
3. _____
4. _____
5. _____
6. _____

Subs:

_____

_____

"teach me to number my days"

24 Hours

SCORE SHEET (Recap of the day)

_____
_____
_____
_____
_____
_____
_____
_____
_____
_____
_____
_____
_____
_____
_____

__Go__ into *__All__* the world, *__Make__* disciples, *__Empowered__* from on high.

Date:_____

SCRIPTURE—What Scripture reference(s) are you reading?

_____

EMPHASIS—What did the Holy Spirit emphasize to you as you read? (If nothing, you haven't read long enough.)

_____
_____
_____
_____
_____
_____

REPENT—What do you need to turn away from so that you may DO what you read?

_____
_____
_____
_____
_____

VOLLEY—What are some ways to share what you've learned with others?

_____
_____

EXPRESS—Express your praise, your confession, your requests to the Lord.

_____
_____
_____
_____
_____
_____
_____
_____
_____
_____
_____
_____

**Go** into **All** the world, **Make** disciples, **Empowered** from on high.

The Lineup

(What needs to be accomplished today?)

1. _____

2. _____

3. _____

4. _____

5. _____

6. _____

Subs:

_____

_____

"teach me to number my days"
24 Hours

SCORE SHEET (Recap of the day)

_____
_____
_____
_____
_____
_____
_____
_____
_____
_____
_____
_____
_____
_____
_____
_____

__Go__ into __All__ the world, __Make__ disciples, __Empowered__ from on high.

Date:_____

SCRIPTURE—What Scripture reference(s) are you reading?

_____

EMPHASIS—What did the Holy Spirit emphasize to you as you read? (If nothing, you haven't read long enough.)

_____
_____
_____
_____
_____
_____

REPENT—What do you need to turn away from so that you may DO what you read?

_____
_____
_____
_____

VOLLEY—What are some ways to share what you've learned with others?

_____
_____

EXPRESS—Express your praise, your confession, your requests to the Lord.

_____
_____
_____
_____
_____
_____
_____
_____
_____
_____
_____

__Go__ into __All__ the world, __Make__ disciples, __Empowered__ from on high.

The Lineup

(What needs to be accomplished today?)

1. _____
2. _____
3. _____
4. _____
5. _____
6. _____

Subs:

_____

_____

"teach me to number my days"

24 Hours

SCORE SHEET (Recap of the day)

_____
_____
_____
_____
_____
_____
_____
_____
_____
_____
_____
_____
_____
_____
_____

__Go__ into __All__ the world, __Make__ disciples, __Empowered__ from on high.

Date:_____

SCRIPTURE—What Scripture reference(s) are you reading?

_____

EMPHASIS—What did the Holy Spirit emphasize to you as you read? (If nothing, you haven't read long enough.)

_____
_____
_____
_____
_____
_____

REPENT—What do you need to turn away from so that you may DO what you read?

_____
_____
_____
_____

VOLLEY—What are some ways to share what you've learned with others?

_____
_____

EXPRESS—Express your praise, your confession, your requests to the Lord.

_____
_____
_____
_____
_____
_____
_____
_____
_____
_____
_____
_____

__Go__ into __All__ the world, __Make__ disciples, __Empowered__ from on high.

The Lineup

(What needs to be accomplished today?)

1. _____

2. _____

3. _____

4. _____

5. _____

6. _____

Subs:

_____

_____

"teach me to number my days"

24 Hours

SCORE SHEET (Recap of the day)

_____
_____
_____
_____
_____
_____
_____
_____
_____
_____
_____
_____
_____
_____

Go into *All* the world, *Make* disciples, *Empowered* from on high.

Date:_____

SCRIPTURE—What Scripture reference(s) are you reading?

_____

EMPHASIS—What did the Holy Spirit emphasize to you as you read? (If nothing, you haven't read long enough.)

_____
_____
_____
_____
_____
_____

REPENT—What do you need to turn away from so that you may DO what you read?

_____
_____
_____
_____
_____

VOLLEY—What are some ways to share what you've learned with others?

_____
_____

EXPRESS—Express your praise, your confession, your requests to the Lord.

_____
_____
_____
_____
_____
_____
_____
_____
_____
_____
_____
_____

_**Go**_ into _**All**_ the world, _**Make**_ disciples, _**Empowered**_ from on high.

The Lineup

(What needs to be accomplished today?)

1. _____
2. _____
3. _____
4. _____
5. _____
6. _____

Subs:

_____

_____

teach me to number my days

24 Hours

SCORE SHEET (Recap of the day)

_____
_____
_____
_____
_____
_____
_____
_____
_____
_____
_____
_____
_____
_____

__Go__ into __All__ the world, __Make__ disciples, __Empowered__ from on high.

Date:_____

SCRIPTURE—What Scripture reference(s) are you reading?

_____

EMPHASIS—What did the Holy Spirit emphasize to you as you read? (If nothing, you haven't read long enough.)

_____
_____
_____
_____
_____
_____

REPENT—What do you need to turn away from so that you may DO what you read?

_____
_____
_____
_____
_____

VOLLEY—What are some ways to share what you've learned with others?

_____
_____

EXPRESS—Express your praise, your confession, your requests to the Lord.

_____
_____
_____
_____
_____
_____
_____
_____
_____
_____
_____
_____
_____

__Go__ into __All__ the world, __Make__ disciples, __Empowered__ from on high.

The Lineup

(What needs to be accomplished today?)

1. _____

2. _____

3. _____

4. _____

5. _____

6. _____

Subs:

_____

_____

"teach me to number my days"

24 Hours

SCORE SHEET (Recap of the day)

_____

_____

_____

_____

_____

_____

_____

_____

_____

_____

_____

_____

_____

_____

_____

__Go__ into __All__ the world, __Make__ disciples, __Empowered__ from on high.

Date:_____

SCRIPTURE—What Scripture reference(s) are you reading?

_____

EMPHASIS—What did the Holy Spirit emphasize to you as you read? (If nothing, you haven't read long enough.)

_____
_____
_____
_____
_____
_____

REPENT—What do you need to turn away from so that you may DO what you read?

_____
_____
_____
_____
_____

VOLLEY—What are some ways to share what you've learned with others?

_____
_____

EXPRESS—Express your praise, your confession, your requests to the Lord.

_____
_____
_____
_____
_____
_____
_____
_____
_____
_____
_____
_____

__Go__ into __All__ the world, __Make__ disciples, __Empowered__ from on high.

The Lineup

(What needs to be accomplished today?)

1. _____

2. _____

3. _____

4. _____

5. _____

6. _____

Subs:

_____

_____

SCORE SHEET (Recap of the day)

_____
_____
_____
_____
_____
_____
_____
_____
_____
_____
_____
_____
_____
_____
_____

Go into *All* the world, *Make* disciples, *Empowered* from on high.

Date:_____

SCRIPTURE—What Scripture reference(s) are you reading?

_____

EMPHASIS—What did the Holy Spirit emphasize to you as you read? (If nothing, you haven't read long enough.)

_____
_____
_____
_____
_____
_____

REPENT—What do you need to turn away from so that you may DO what you read?

_____
_____
_____
_____
_____

VOLLEY—What are some ways to share what you've learned with others?

_____
_____

EXPRESS—Express your praise, your confession, your requests to the Lord.

_____
_____
_____
_____
_____
_____
_____
_____
_____
_____
_____
_____

__Go__ into __All__ the world, __Make__ disciples, __Empowered__ from on high.

The Lineup

(What needs to be accomplished today?)

1. _____

2. _____

3. _____

4. _____

5. _____

6. _____

Subs:

_____

_____

"teach me to number my days"

24 Hours

SCORE SHEET (Recap of the day)

_____

_____

_____

_____

_____

_____

_____

_____

_____

_____

_____

_____

_____

_____

Go into ***All*** the world, ***Make*** disciples, ***Empowered*** from on high.

Date:_____

SCRIPTURE—What Scripture reference(s) are you reading?

_____

EMPHASIS—What did the Holy Spirit emphasize to you as you read? (If nothing, you haven't read long enough.)

_____
_____
_____
_____
_____
_____

REPENT—What do you need to turn away from so that you may DO what you read?

_____
_____
_____
_____
_____

VOLLEY—What are some ways to share what you've learned with others?

_____
_____

EXPRESS—Express your praise, your confession, your requests to the Lord.

_____
_____
_____
_____
_____
_____
_____
_____
_____
_____
_____
_____

__Go__ into __All__ the world, __Make__ disciples, __Empowered__ from on high.

The Lineup

(What needs to be accomplished today?)

1. _____
2. _____
3. _____
4. _____
5. _____
6. _____

Subs:

_____

_____

"teach me to number my days"

24 Hours

SCORE SHEET (Recap of the day)

_____
_____
_____
_____
_____
_____
_____
_____
_____
_____
_____
_____
_____
_____
_____
_____

Go into ***All*** the world, ***Make*** disciples, ***Empowered*** from on high.

Date:_____

SCRIPTURE—What Scripture reference(s) are you reading?

_____

EMPHASIS—What did the Holy Spirit emphasize to you as you read? (If nothing, you haven't read long enough.)

_____
_____
_____
_____
_____
_____

REPENT—What do you need to turn away from so that you may DO what you read?

_____
_____
_____
_____
_____

VOLLEY—What are some ways to share what you've learned with others?

_____
_____

EXPRESS—Express your praise, your confession, your requests to the Lord.

_____
_____
_____
_____
_____
_____
_____
_____
_____
_____
_____
_____

__Go__ into __All__ the world, __Make__ disciples, __Empowered__ from on high.

The Lineup

(What needs to be accomplished today?)

1. _____
2. _____
3. _____
4. _____
5. _____
6. _____

Subs:

_____

_____

"teach me to number my days"

24 Hours

SCORE SHEET (Recap of the day)

_____
_____
_____
_____
_____
_____
_____
_____
_____
_____
_____
_____
_____
_____

***Go** into **All** the world, **Make** disciples, **Empowered** from on high.*

Date:_____

SCRIPTURE—What Scripture reference(s) are you reading?

_____

EMPHASIS—What did the Holy Spirit emphasize to you as you read? (If nothing, you haven't read long enough.)

_____
_____
_____
_____
_____
_____

REPENT—What do you need to turn away from so that you may DO what you read?

_____
_____
_____
_____
_____

VOLLEY—What are some ways to share what you've learned with others?

_____
_____
_____

EXPRESS—Express your praise, your confession, your requests to the Lord.

_____
_____
_____
_____
_____
_____
_____
_____
_____
_____
_____
_____

__Go__ into __All__ the world, __Make__ disciples, __Empowered__ from on high.

The Lineup

(What needs to be accomplished today?)

1. _____

2. _____

3. _____

4. _____

5. _____

6. _____

Subs:

_____

_____

"teach me to number my days"

24 Hours

SCORE SHEET (Recap of the day)

__Go__ into __All__ the world, __Make__ disciples, __Empowered__ from on high.

Date:_____

SCRIPTURE—What Scripture reference(s) are you reading?

_____

EMPHASIS—What did the Holy Spirit emphasize to you as you read? (If nothing, you haven't read long enough.)

_____
_____
_____
_____
_____
_____

REPENT—What do you need to turn away from so that you may DO what you read?

_____
_____
_____
_____
_____

VOLLEY—What are some ways to share what you've learned with others?

_____
_____

EXPRESS—Express your praise, your confession, your requests to the Lord.

_____
_____
_____
_____
_____
_____
_____
_____
_____
_____
_____
_____

__G__o into *__All__* the world, *__Make__* disciples, *__Empowered__* from on high.

The Lineup

(What needs to be accomplished today?)

1. _____
2. _____
3. _____
4. _____
5. _____
6. _____

Subs:

_____

_____

"teach me to number my days"

24 Hours

SCORE SHEET (Recap of the day)

_____
_____
_____
_____
_____
_____
_____
_____
_____
_____
_____
_____
_____
_____

__Go__ into __All__ the world, __Make__ disciples, __Empowered__ from on high.

Date:_____

SCRIPTURE—What Scripture reference(s) are you reading?

_____

EMPHASIS—What did the Holy Spirit emphasize to you as you read? (If nothing, you haven't read long enough.)

_____
_____
_____
_____
_____
_____

REPENT—What do you need to turn away from so that you may DO what you read?

_____
_____
_____
_____
_____

VOLLEY—What are some ways to share what you've learned with others?

_____
_____

EXPRESS—Express your praise, your confession, your requests to the Lord.

_____
_____
_____
_____
_____
_____
_____
_____
_____
_____
_____
_____

**Go** into **All** the world, **Make** disciples, **Empowered** from on high.

The Lineup

(What needs to be accomplished today?)

1. _____
2. _____
3. _____
4. _____
5. _____
6. _____

Subs:

_____

_____

"teach me to number my days"

24 Hours

SCORE SHEET (Recap of the day)

_____
_____
_____
_____
_____
_____
_____
_____
_____
_____
_____
_____
_____
_____
_____
_____

__Go__ into __All__ the world, __Make__ disciples, __Empowered__ from on high.

Date:_____

Scripture—What Scripture reference(s) are you reading?

_____

Emphasis—What did the Holy Spirit emphasize to you as you read? (If nothing, you haven't read long enough.)

_____
_____
_____
_____
_____
_____

Repent—What do you need to turn away from so that you may DO what you read?

_____
_____
_____
_____
_____

Volley—What are some ways to share what you've learned with others?

_____
_____

Express—Express your praise, your confession, your requests to the Lord.

_____
_____
_____
_____
_____
_____
_____
_____
_____
_____
_____
_____

__Go__ into __All__ the world, __Make__ disciples, __Empowered__ from on high.

The Lineup

(What needs to be accomplished today?)

1. _____
2. _____
3. _____
4. _____
5. _____
6. _____

Subs:

_____

_____

"teach me to number my days"

24 Hours

SCORE SHEET (Recap of the day)

_____
_____
_____
_____
_____
_____
_____
_____
_____
_____
_____
_____
_____
_____
_____

__Go__ into __All__ the world, __Make__ disciples, __Empowered__ from on high.

Date:_____

Scripture—What Scripture reference(s) are you reading?

_____

Emphasis—What did the Holy Spirit emphasize to you as you read? (If nothing, you haven't read long enough.)

_____
_____
_____
_____
_____
_____

Repent—What do you need to turn away from so that you may DO what you read?

_____
_____
_____
_____

Volley—What are some ways to share what you've learned with others?

_____
_____

Express—Express your praise, your confession, your requests to the Lord.

_____
_____
_____
_____
_____
_____
_____
_____
_____
_____
_____

__Go__ into __All__ the world, __Make__ disciples, __Empowered__ from on high.

The Lineup

(What needs to be accomplished today?)

1. _____

2. _____

3. _____

4. _____

5. _____

6. _____

Subs:

_____

_____

"teach me to number my days"

24 Hours

SCORE SHEET (Recap of the day)

_____
_____
_____
_____
_____
_____
_____
_____
_____
_____
_____
_____
_____
_____

__Go__ into __All__ the world, __Make__ disciples, __Empowered__ from on high.

Date:_____

SCRIPTURE—What Scripture reference(s) are you reading?

_____

EMPHASIS—What did the Holy Spirit emphasize to you as you read? (If nothing, you haven't read long enough.)

_____
_____
_____
_____
_____
_____

REPENT—What do you need to turn away from so that you may DO what you read?

_____
_____
_____
_____
_____

VOLLEY—What are some ways to share what you've learned with others?

_____
_____

EXPRESS—Express your praise, your confession, your requests to the Lord.

_____
_____
_____
_____
_____
_____
_____
_____
_____
_____
_____

__Go__ into __All__ the world, __Make__ disciples, __Empowered__ from on high.

The Lineup

(What needs to be accomplished today?)

1. _____
2. _____
3. _____
4. _____
5. _____
6. _____

Subs:

_____

_____

"teach me to number my days"

24 Hours

SCORE SHEET (Recap of the day)

_____
_____
_____
_____
_____
_____
_____
_____
_____
_____
_____
_____
_____
_____

*<u>**Go**</u> into <u>**All**</u> the world, <u>**Make**</u> disciples, <u>**Empowered**</u> from on high.*

Date:_____

SCRIPTURE—What Scripture reference(s) are you reading?

_____

EMPHASIS—What did the Holy Spirit emphasize to you as you read? (If nothing, you haven't read long enough.)

_____
_____
_____
_____
_____
_____

REPENT—What do you need to turn away from so that you may DO what you read?

_____
_____
_____
_____
_____

VOLLEY—What are some ways to share what you've learned with others?

_____
_____

EXPRESS—Express your praise, your confession, your requests to the Lord.

_____
_____
_____
_____
_____
_____
_____
_____
_____
_____
_____
_____

Go into *All* the world, *Make* disciples, *Empowered* from on high.

The Lineup

(What needs to be accomplished today?)

1. _____
2. _____
3. _____
4. _____
5. _____
6. _____

Subs:

_____

_____

"teach me to number my days"

24 Hours

SCORE SHEET (Recap of the day)

_____
_____
_____
_____
_____
_____
_____
_____
_____
_____
_____
_____
_____
_____
_____

__Go__ into __All__ the world, __Make__ disciples, __Empowered__ from on high.

Date:_____

SCRIPTURE—What Scripture reference(s) are you reading?

_____

EMPHASIS—What did the Holy Spirit emphasize to you as you read? (If nothing, you haven't read long enough.)

_____
_____
_____
_____
_____
_____

REPENT—What do you need to turn away from so that you may DO what you read?

_____
_____
_____
_____
_____

VOLLEY—What are some ways to share what you've learned with others?

_____
_____

EXPRESS—Express your praise, your confession, your requests to the Lord.

_____
_____
_____
_____
_____
_____
_____
_____
_____
_____
_____

**Go** into **All** the world, **Make** disciples, **Empowered** from on high.

The Lineup

(What needs to be accomplished today?)

1. _____
2. _____
3. _____
4. _____
5. _____
6. _____

Subs:

_____

_____

"teach me to number my days"

24 Hours

SCORE SHEET (Recap of the day)

_____
_____
_____
_____
_____
_____
_____
_____
_____
_____
_____
_____
_____
_____
_____
_____

__Go__ into __All__ the world, __Make__ disciples, __Empowered__ from on high.

Date:_____

SCRIPTURE—What Scripture reference(s) are you reading?

_____

EMPHASIS—What did the Holy Spirit emphasize to you as you read? (If nothing, you haven't read long enough.)

_____
_____
_____
_____
_____
_____

REPENT—What do you need to turn away from so that you may DO what you read?

_____
_____
_____
_____
_____

VOLLEY—What are some ways to share what you've learned with others?

_____
_____

EXPRESS—Express your praise, your confession, your requests to the Lord.

_____
_____
_____
_____
_____
_____
_____
_____
_____
_____
_____
_____

__Go__ into __All__ the world, __Make__ disciples, __Empowered__ from on high.

The Lineup

(What needs to be accomplished today?)

1. _____

2. _____

3. _____

4. _____

5. _____

6. _____

Subs:

_____

_____

"teach me to number my days"

24 Hours

SCORE SHEET (Recap of the day)

_____

_____

_____

_____

_____

_____

_____

_____

_____

_____

_____

_____

_____

_____

_____

__Go__ into __All__ the world, __Make__ disciples, __Empowered__ from on high.

Date:_____

SCRIPTURE—What Scripture reference(s) are you reading?

_____

EMPHASIS—What did the Holy Spirit emphasize to you as you read? (If nothing, you haven't read long enough.)

_____
_____
_____
_____
_____
_____

REPENT—What do you need to turn away from so that you may DO what you read?

_____
_____
_____
_____

VOLLEY—What are some ways to share what you've learned with others?

_____
_____

EXPRESS—Express your praise, your confession, your requests to the Lord.

_____
_____
_____
_____
_____
_____
_____
_____
_____
_____
_____

__Go__ into __All__ the world, __Make__ disciples, __Empowered__ from on high.

The Lineup

(What needs to be accomplished today?)

1. _____
2. _____
3. _____
4. _____
5. _____
6. _____

Subs:

_____

_____

"teach me to number my days"

24 Hours

SCORE SHEET (Recap of the day)

_____
_____
_____
_____
_____
_____
_____
_____
_____
_____
_____
_____
_____
_____
_____

**Go** into **All** the world, **Make** disciples, **Empowered** from on high.

Date:_____

SCRIPTURE—What Scripture reference(s) are you reading?

_____

EMPHASIS—What did the Holy Spirit emphasize to you as you read? (If nothing, you haven't read long enough.)

_____
_____
_____
_____
_____
_____

REPENT—What do you need to turn away from so that you may DO what you read?

_____
_____
_____
_____
_____

VOLLEY—What are some ways to share what you've learned with others?

_____
_____

EXPRESS—Express your praise, your confession, your requests to the Lord.

_____
_____
_____
_____
_____
_____
_____
_____
_____
_____
_____

<u>G</u>o into *<u>A</u>ll* the world, ***Make*** disciples, ***Empowered*** from on high.

The Lineup

(What needs to be accomplished today?)

1. _____

2. _____

3. _____

4. _____

5. _____

6. _____

Subs:

_____

_____

"teach me to number my days"

24 Hours

SCORE SHEET (Recap of the day)

_____

_____

_____

_____

_____

_____

_____

_____

_____

_____

_____

_____

_____

_____

_____

__Go__ into __All__ the world, __Make__ disciples, __Empowered__ from on high.

Date:_____

SCRIPTURE—What Scripture reference(s) are you reading?

_____

EMPHASIS—What did the Holy Spirit emphasize to you as you read? (If nothing, you haven't read long enough.)

_____
_____
_____
_____
_____
_____

REPENT—What do you need to turn away from so that you may DO what you read?

_____
_____
_____
_____
_____

VOLLEY—What are some ways to share what you've learned with others?

_____
_____

EXPRESS—Express your praise, your confession, your requests to the Lord.

_____
_____
_____
_____
_____
_____
_____
_____
_____
_____
_____

Go into *All* the world, *Make* disciples, *Empowered* from on high.

The Lineup

(What needs to be accomplished today?)

1. _____
2. _____
3. _____
4. _____
5. _____
6. _____

Subs:

_____

_____

"teach me to number my days"

24 Hours

SCORE SHEET (Recap of the day)

_____
_____
_____
_____
_____
_____
_____
_____
_____
_____
_____
_____
_____
_____
_____
_____

**Go** into **All** the world, **Make** disciples, **Empowered** from on high.

Date:_____

SCRIPTURE—What Scripture reference(s) are you reading?

_____

EMPHASIS—What did the Holy Spirit emphasize to you as you read? (If nothing, you haven't read long enough.)

_____
_____
_____
_____
_____
_____

REPENT—What do you need to turn away from so that you may DO what you read?

_____
_____
_____
_____
_____

VOLLEY—What are some ways to share what you've learned with others?

_____
_____

EXPRESS—Express your praise, your confession, your requests to the Lord.

_____
_____
_____
_____
_____
_____
_____
_____
_____
_____
_____
_____

*<u>G</u>o into <u>All</u> the world, <u>**Make**</u> disciples, <u>**Empowered**</u> from on high.*

The Lineup

(What needs to be accomplished today?)

1. _____
2. _____
3. _____
4. _____
5. _____
6. _____

Subs:

_____

_____

"teach me to number my days"

24 Hours

SCORE SHEET (Recap of the day)

_____
_____
_____
_____
_____
_____
_____
_____
_____
_____
_____
_____
_____
_____
_____
_____

__Go__ into __All__ the world, __Make__ disciples, __Empowered__ from on high.

Date:_____

SCRIPTURE—What Scripture reference(s) are you reading?

_____

EMPHASIS—What did the Holy Spirit emphasize to you as you read? (If nothing, you haven't read long enough.)

_____
_____
_____
_____
_____
_____

REPENT—What do you need to turn away from so that you may DO what you read?

_____
_____
_____
_____
_____

VOLLEY—What are some ways to share what you've learned with others?

_____
_____

EXPRESS—Express your praise, your confession, your requests to the Lord.

_____
_____
_____
_____
_____
_____
_____
_____
_____
_____
_____

__Go__ into __All__ the world, __Make__ disciples, __Empowered__ from on high.

The Lineup

(What needs to be accomplished today?)

1. _____
2. _____
3. _____
4. _____
5. _____
6. _____

Subs:

_____

_____

"teach me to number my days"

24 Hours

SCORE SHEET (Recap of the day)

_____
_____
_____
_____
_____
_____
_____
_____
_____
_____
_____
_____
_____
_____
_____

__Go__ into __All__ the world, __Make__ disciples, __Empowered__ from on high.

Date:_____

SCRIPTURE—What Scripture reference(s) are you reading?

_____

EMPHASIS—What did the Holy Spirit emphasize to you as you read? (If nothing, you haven't read long enough.)

_____
_____
_____
_____
_____
_____

REPENT—What do you need to turn away from so that you may DO what you read?

_____
_____
_____
_____

VOLLEY—What are some ways to share what you've learned with others?

_____
_____

EXPRESS—Express your praise, your confession, your requests to the Lord.

_____
_____
_____
_____
_____
_____
_____
_____
_____
_____
_____

__Go__ into __All__ the world, __Make__ disciples, __Empowered__ from on high.

The Lineup

(What needs to be accomplished today?)

1. _____

2. _____

3. _____

4. _____

5. _____

6. _____

Subs:

_____

_____

"teach me to number my days"

24 Hours

SCORE SHEET (Recap of the day)

_____
_____
_____
_____
_____
_____
_____
_____
_____
_____
_____
_____
_____
_____

__Go__ into __All__ the world, __Make__ disciples, __Empowered__ from on high.

Date:_____

SCRIPTURE—What Scripture reference(s) are you reading?

_____

EMPHASIS—What did the Holy Spirit emphasize to you as you read? (If nothing, you haven't read long enough.)

_____
_____
_____
_____
_____
_____

REPENT—What do you need to turn away from so that you may DO what you read?

_____
_____
_____
_____
_____

VOLLEY—What are some ways to share what you've learned with others?

_____
_____

EXPRESS—Express your praise, your confession, your requests to the Lord.

_____
_____
_____
_____
_____
_____
_____
_____
_____
_____
_____

__Go__ into __All__ the world, __Make__ disciples, __Empowered__ from on high.

The Lineup

(What needs to be accomplished today?)

1. _____
2. _____
3. _____
4. _____
5. _____
6. _____

Subs:

_____

_____

"teach me to number my days"

24 Hours

SCORE SHEET (Recap of the day)

_____

_____

_____

_____

_____

_____

_____

_____

_____

_____

_____

_____

_____

_____

__Go__ into __All__ the world, __Make__ disciples, __Empowered__ from on high.

Date:_____

SCRIPTURE—What Scripture reference(s) are you reading?

_____

EMPHASIS—What did the Holy Spirit emphasize to you as you read? (If nothing, you haven't read long enough.)

_____
_____
_____
_____
_____
_____

REPENT—What do you need to turn away from so that you may DO what you read?

_____
_____
_____
_____
_____

VOLLEY—What are some ways to share what you've learned with others?

_____
_____

EXPRESS—Express your praise, your confession, your requests to the Lord.

_____
_____
_____
_____
_____
_____
_____
_____
_____
_____
_____

__Go__ into __All__ the world, __Make__ disciples, __Empowered__ from on high.

The Lineup

(What needs to be accomplished today?)

1. _____

2. _____

3. _____

4. _____

5. _____

6. _____

Subs:

_____

_____

"teach me to number my days"

24 Hours

SCORE SHEET (Recap of the day)

_____

_____

_____

_____

_____

_____

_____

_____

_____

_____

_____

_____

_____

_____

__Go__ into __All__ the world, __Make__ disciples, __Empowered__ from on high.

Date:_____

SCRIPTURE—What Scripture reference(s) are you reading?

_____

EMPHASIS—What did the Holy Spirit emphasize to you as you read? (If nothing, you haven't read long enough.)

_____
_____
_____
_____
_____
_____

REPENT—What do you need to turn away from so that you may DO what you read?

_____
_____
_____
_____
_____

VOLLEY—What are some ways to share what you've learned with others?

_____
_____

EXPRESS—Express your praise, your confession, your requests to the Lord.

_____
_____
_____
_____
_____
_____
_____
_____
_____
_____
_____

__Go__ into __All__ the world, __Make__ disciples, __Empowered__ from on high.

The Lineup

(What needs to be accomplished today?)

1. _____
2. _____
3. _____
4. _____
5. _____
6. _____

Subs:

_____

_____

"teach me to number my days"

24 Hours

SCORE SHEET (Recap of the day)

_____
_____
_____
_____
_____
_____
_____
_____
_____
_____
_____
_____
_____
_____
_____
_____

__Go__ into __All__ the world, __Make__ disciples, __Empowered__ from on high.

Date:_____

SCRIPTURE—What Scripture reference(s) are you reading?

_____

EMPHASIS—What did the Holy Spirit emphasize to you as you read? (If nothing, you haven't read long enough.)

_____
_____
_____
_____
_____
_____

REPENT—What do you need to turn away from so that you may DO what you read?

_____
_____
_____
_____

VOLLEY—What are some ways to share what you've learned with others?

_____
_____

EXPRESS—Express your praise, your confession, your requests to the Lord.

_____
_____
_____
_____
_____
_____
_____
_____
_____
_____

__Go__ into *__All__* the world, *__Make__* disciples, *__Empowered__* from on high.

The Lineup

(What needs to be accomplished today?)

1. _____

2. _____

3. _____

4. _____

5. _____

6. _____

Subs:

_____

_____

"teach me to number my days"

24 Hours

SCORE SHEET (Recap of the day)

_____

_____

_____

_____

_____

_____

_____

_____

_____

_____

_____

_____

_____

_____

_____

__Go__ into __All__ the world, __Make__ disciples, __Empowered__ from on high.

Date:_____

SCRIPTURE—What Scripture reference(s) are you reading?

_____

EMPHASIS—What did the Holy Spirit emphasize to you as you read? (If nothing, you haven't read long enough.)

_____
_____
_____
_____
_____
_____

REPENT—What do you need to turn away from so that you may DO what you read?

_____
_____
_____
_____

VOLLEY—What are some ways to share what you've learned with others?

_____
_____

EXPRESS—Express your praise, your confession, your requests to the Lord.

_____
_____
_____
_____
_____
_____
_____
_____
_____
_____
_____

**Go** into **All** the world, **Make** disciples, **Empowered** from on high.

The Lineup

(What needs to be accomplished today?)

1. _____

2. _____

3. _____

4. _____

5. _____

6. _____

Subs:

_____

_____

"teach me to number my days"

24 Hours

SCORE SHEET (Recap of the day)

_____
_____
_____
_____
_____
_____
_____
_____
_____
_____
_____
_____
_____
_____
_____

__Go__ into __All__ the world, __Make__ disciples, __Empowered__ from on high.

Date:_____

SCRIPTURE—What Scripture reference(s) are you reading?

_____

EMPHASIS—What did the Holy Spirit emphasize to you as you read? (If nothing, you haven't read long enough.)

_____
_____
_____
_____
_____
_____

REPENT—What do you need to turn away from so that you may DO what you read?

_____
_____
_____
_____
_____

VOLLEY—What are some ways to share what you've learned with others?

_____
_____

EXPRESS—Express your praise, your confession, your requests to the Lord.

_____
_____
_____
_____
_____
_____
_____
_____
_____
_____
_____

Go into *All* the world, *Make* disciples, *Empowered* from on high.

The Lineup

(What needs to be accomplished today?)

1. _____

2. _____

3. _____

4. _____

5. _____

6. _____

Subs:

_____

_____

"teach me to number my days"

24 Hours

SCORE SHEET (Recap of the day)

_____
_____
_____
_____
_____
_____
_____
_____
_____
_____
_____
_____
_____
_____

About the Author

Jackie Taylor believes sports and the Bible go hand-in-hand to help athletes and coaches prepare for the challenges and opportunities they face on and off the field of play. She provides sports mentoring services, coach and player Bible studies, and resources to help athletes become who God has designed them to be.

Jackie has coached teams for over 15 years. She has been an FCA team chaplain for eight years.

She has a Bachelor's Degree in Communications from the University of Alabama.

For more information, visit coachjaytee.com.

Made in the USA
Middletown, DE
02 October 2017